The Harmony
of
Goodness

The Harmony of Goodness

Mutuality and Moral Living
According to John Duns Scotus

by

Mary Beth Ingham, CSJ

Franciscan Press

The Harmony of Goodness: Mutuality and Moral Living
According to John Duns Scotus
Mary Elizabeth Ingham, C.S.J.

Franciscan Press
Quincy University
1800 College Avenue
Quincy, IL 62301
ph 217.228.5670
fax 217.228.5672

Book design, cover design and typesetting by Laurel Fitch, Chicago, IL.
Cover painting and calligraphy by Madeleva Williams, C.S.J.

Printed in the United States of America
First Printing: January 1996
0 1 2 3 4 5 6 7 8 9

Library of Congress Cataloging-in-Publication Data
Ingham, Mary Elizabeth, 1951–
    The harmony of goodness : mutuality and moral living according to John Duns
Scotus / by Mary Elizabeth Ingham.
            p.   cm.
    Includes bibliographical references and indexes.
    ISBN 0-8199-0969-6 (alk. paper)
    1. Duns Scotus, John, ca. 1266-1308 -- Ethics. 2. Ethics, Medieval. 3. Christian ethics
-- History -- Middle Ages, 600-1500. I. Title.
    B765.D74I55 1996   95-51539
    171'.2'092--dc20   CIP

To my family, with gratitude

Contents

Preface

The closing years of the 20th century have been an important time for the study of medieval thought. The rediscovery of key insights, the development of techniques and methods for study of manuscripts, the publication of critical editions: all these elements have contributed to a better understanding of the philosophical insights and historical context within the period called the Middle Ages, between the 9th and the 15th centuries. The philosophers and theologians of the 13th century, in particular, offer a vision of human nature and fulfillment which is both integrated and focused on the value of the created order. They are optimistic about the human capacity for knowledge and love. They are confident that divine grace is present in all reality.

Among these thinkers stands John Duns Scotus, the "Subtle Doctor," who until recently figured only as a medieval afterthought to his more well-known Dominican predecessor, Thomas Aquinas. Scotist thought enjoys something of a renaissance today, as medievalists rediscover and unpack the specifically Franciscan dimension of his insights on the value of creation, the importance of divine and human freedom and the primacy of love. Scotus's vision is not limited to those who follow the Rule of St. Francis. His is truly an ecumenical spirit which seeks to discern within reality the traces of divine love. The present book is my contribution toward the rediscovery of the values in Scotist thought for today, and particularly as they relate to moral living.

This study began as an article for the *American Catholic Philosophical Quarterly*. It developed thanks to numerous research grants from

Loyola Marymount University since 1992. Its final form is the result of a University Fellowship for Spring Semester 1995. In addition, several colleagues have assisted me with their comments and suggestions. In particular, I am grateful to the kindness of Allan B. Wolter, OFM who has taken such interest in my studies on Scotus and to Marilyn McCord Adams who offered helpful insights on an earlier version of this book. I would also like to thank Linda Zagzebski for her discussions of chapters 4 and 5. Jim Hanink and Susan Rabe were kind enough to read the final manuscript and offer suggestions. This book would never have come to completion without the support and encouragement of my Franciscan friends, Edward Coughlin, OFM, Director of the Franciscan Institute, Kathleen Moffatt, OSF and Dorothy McCormick, OSF, whose lived experience of the spirituality of Francis and Clare offers me the opportunity to see how Scotist insights reflect this important tradition. Finally, I am most grateful for the support of my own religious community, the Sisters of St. Joseph of Orange and especially the support of the Sisters with whom I live.

Los Angeles, California
March 19, 1995

Introduction

John Duns Scotus belongs to the second generation of philosopher-theologians who worked to integrate Aristotelian insights with Christian revelation (*sacra doctrina*). Writing after the Condemnations of 1277 (Paris) and 1284 (Oxford), Scotus pursued a relentless analysis of the legacy of Greek thought available to Latin thinkers at the close of the 13th century, thanks to the translations of such scholars as Robert Grosseteste and William of Moerbeke. This analysis required the appropriate understanding and separation of Aristotelian thought from that of the Arab commentaries, such as those of Avicenna and Averroes, whose interpretations of the Stagirite fueled the developing autonomy of the Masters in the Faculty of Arts and threatened the primacy of theology at the University of Paris.

Before his untimely death in the autumn of 1308, Scotus succeeded in effectively rethinking the relationship between philosophy and theology in light of a deeper understanding of Aristotle as well as a concern to safeguard key elements of Christian revelation: the possibility for free choice in the will, the contingency of creation and the value of theology as a scientific discipline. This rethinking involved a serious and critical rejection of the necessitarian world-view which had emerged from the Arab philosophers and a clear defense of the centrality of freedom, both divine and human, as the cornerstone of the Christian understanding of reality.[1] Because of his early death at the age of 42,

---

[1] For more on this and its influence on Scotus, see Roland Hissette, *Enquête sur*

Scotus was unable to produce the sort of textual synthesis for which Thomas Aquinas is famous.

Why would anyone want to read or study Duns Scotus today? What has a medieval thinker to contribute to our contemporary moral discussion? There are surely many aspects of medieval culture we would not want to re-introduce into contemporary moral or social discussion. There are, however, several elements within the medieval worldview and within Scotus's moral vision which make him attractive for study today.

First, we live in an age where old paradigms are falling asunder. No longer does the world appear as it did even ten years ago. The East-West configuration is gone and the renewed political and social orders call for new ways of dealing with reality around us. We must find a new framework from which to confront the issues facing us into the 21st century. Such a perspective may indeed be found from the wealth of tradition and spiritual resources of Christianity.

Second, Scotus possesses several qualities which make him attractive. As a Franciscan, he is deeply committed to the value of creation and to our relationship with all that exists. As a theologian, he exhibits very positive attitudes toward women, both in the inclusive imagery he uses when speaking of God and his focus on Mary as sinless model of human perfection. As a medieval writer within Latin Christianity, he is conscious of the effects of original sin upon the human response to God. Despite this awareness, Scotus separates human sinfulness from God's response in the Covenant with the Jews and particularly in the Incarnation. Scotus rejects out of hand the famous argument of Anselm, in which the Bishop of Canterbury places the Incarnation within the context of payment for the sin of Adam and Eve. For the Franciscan, the birth of Jesus was ordained by God prior to creation and, thus, prior to sin. There is no repayment of an infinite debt for which Jesus had to be born or to be sacrificed. The center for Scotus's

---

les 219 articles condamnés à Paris le 7 mars 1277, Louvain-Paris 1977; Fernand van Steenberghen, "La philosophie à la veille de l'entrée en scène de Jean Duns Scot" in *De Doctrina I. Duns Scoti*, I:65-74; Paul Vignaux, "Valeur morale et valeur de salut" in *Homo et mundus*, 53-67. I discuss a direct influence upon Scotus's ethical discussion in "The Condemnation of 1277: Another Light on Scotist Ethics" in *Freiburger Zeitschrift für Theologie und Philosophie*, 37 (1990), 91-103.

discussion of moral living is not sin but Christ, the fullest expression of God's infinite love.

Third, Scotus moves beyond a bi-polar presentation of issues and seeks to harmonize various aspects of a situation to discover the truth beneath the differing positions. His is an approach which is reconciling: bringing together internal and external realms, human and divine activity, natural and graced living. In Scotus we discover an integrated presentation of what *human* really might mean. This reflects the medieval predilection for a vision of the whole which underpins their optimism about human nature and moral living. To study Scotus is to enter a challenging realm where the intellectual and spiritual come together, where the mind and heart are not opposed but rather seek together the fullness of life.

In this book I attempt a presentation of Scotus which is at once accessible and consonant with the depth of his thinking. This will not always produce a clear and concise discussion. Scotus does not present a perspective which can be reduced to easy schema and mathematical formula. He seeks to represent reality as it is, with all the intricacy of life and the beauty of organic dynamism. This means that sometimes the discussion will turn to a more technical presentation of distinctions necessary for us to understand the depth of beauty Scotus presents. These more technical sections are balanced with concrete examples. Together, the specialized and ordinary dimensions of this book reveal the mystery of human life: with its sophisticated and unsophisticated elements, all reality reveals God.

One discussion of particular density appears in chapter 1, when we consider Scotus's understanding of the relationships among the Persons in the Trinity. While there are those who might consider such a specialized discussion beyond the scope of most readers, it is an essential point in understanding Scotus's moral vision. His presentation of the Trinity as Persons in relationship offers the basis for mutuality which I identify as central to his moral perspective. In order to have a relationship, one must have individuals capable of relating to one another as distinct individuals. In this way, Trinitarian communion not only models the family community, but also the social order. According to Scotus, society is meant to be individuals in communion, seeking the common good.

To grasp the manner by which Scotus understands the divine and human realms in a more dynamic way, I have chosen an image common to most everyday life. This image is not static, but a moving and beautiful decoration often found in a garden. This decoration exhibits both visual and musical harmony. It is a wind chime. Five ceramic figures hang from a single point, separated by a large disk. Each figure is parallel to the others and joined to them by means of the string or wire which holds the chime together. No piece touches the others, each is separate and distinct as an individual part of the whole configuration. From the large disk at the top hangs a smaller disk which balances the entire chime. Perhaps it is decorated with a colorful tassle or other ornament. Sometimes it is hidden by the other figures. Yet this small disk holds the secret to the music of the chime. When the wind blows, the small disk is moved to strike one figure, then another. Soon all the figures are in movement, striking each other and dancing in the wind. The dance is beautiful to see. It is also beautiful to hear, for the figures produce the music which accompanies their dance. The harmony of musical sounds coming from a wind chime is not a tune that one could whistle. It is a quiet song created by the fragility of the figures, the balance of the pieces and the harmony of their interaction. It is an aesthetic whole which pleases both eye and ear.

I have chosen this image because Scotus offers an aesthetic framework for moral living. The artistic dimension to his thinking has both visual and musical elements. The moral act constitutes a whole where all aspects fit together. Balance and harmony are important to the moral goal. Part of my own reading of Scotus has been informed by his concern to speak of the morally good act as a beautiful work of art, and of the moral agent as a formed artist. I examine the moral philosophy of John Duns Scotus as if it were a wind chime: composed of several independent elements, all interrelated in such a way that their mutual interaction produces the harmony which is goodness. The Scotist understanding of moral living is based upon the mutuality of all parts within a balanced and harmonious whole. The moral paradigm or configuration he presents is intricate and dynamic. It must be studied from several viewpoints in order to appreciate its integrated beauty. Just as we would walk around a wind chime to admire its construction and balance, so we shall *walk around* Scotus's paradigm to admire the balance and harmony with which this 13th century Franciscan describes and discusses the beauty of human living and its ultimate expression in love. In each chapter I focus on a different aspect of the whole moral framework, and in each chapter the whole will appear to us from a slightly different vantage point.

I attempt to focus on smaller elements without losing the sense of the whole. This will not be easy, since Scotus's attention to detail can often mask his understanding of how the entirety of human living fits together. While earlier chapters may give the impression of fragmentation, later chapters will work to integrate the discussion into the harmonic whole which is typical of Scotus.

What are the pieces of this vision? How does Scotus construct his wind chime? At the center, of course, is the freedom which characterizes all human action. The ability to choose freely, after proper deliberation, constitutes the uniquely *human* quality of moral living. Just as the center disk of any chime is weighted so that it hangs properly and can properly strike the other pieces, so too human freedom within the will carries the weight which Scotus identifies as love. Following Augustine, he affirms that the human heart is drawn in and by love, just as a stone is drawn toward the earth by the force of its weight. Love draws us in our choices. Our need for love and desire to love is the source of our actions. Love completes our actions in the creation of relationships with others and, especially, with God.

Around the center piece hang the other elements of the model: the value of the person as basis for moral living, the object of the will's longing, moral goodness as a harmonic configuration, the importance of virtue as aid in moral choices, the notion of right reasoning as artistic discernment, and finally, the order of merit as relationship with God. Each chapter focuses on one aspect of these and seeks to present the others from its perspective. At the conclusion, we may have a deeper understanding of the entire vision as the combined configuration of all the pieces and their interrelationships.

The wind which blows through this wind chime is the wind of the Spirit, and no understanding of Scotus is possible without some attention to the spiritual tradition within which he writes. It is a dynamic tradition whose roots reach back to the Eastern tradition within Christianity and whose insights arise from an understanding of the human person as image of God. This tradition sees human living as a process of divinization within which human and divine persons work together to produce goodness, within which there is no rift between the natural and so-called supernatural realms and within which creation is a gift, graced and blessed by a loving God.

John Duns Scotus was born in Duns, Scotland in the spring of 1265. He entered the newly founded Franciscan mendicant order as a young

man, possibly even in his early teens. Ordained in 1291, Scotus was edu-
cated in Scotland and Oxford, before travelling to Paris to finish his
education and receive the degree of Master in Theology (around the
year 1305). His years of study took place during a period of political and
ecclesiastical hostility between King Philip the Fair of France and Pope
Boniface VIII. In June of 1303 Scotus was forced into exile for failure to
support the King in his efforts to depose the Pope. At this point his
whereabouts are uncertain, but the best scholarly guess puts him in
Oxford until April 1304, when he was able to resume his lecturing in
Paris. After being named Regent Master in Paris (1305), Scotus was sent
to Cologne in 1307 to take charge of the education of the newer members in the House of Studies. He died there quite unexpectedly on
November 8, at the very young age of 42, and is buried in the Franciscan
church (*Minoritenkirche*) near the Cologne cathedral.

Scotus's early death accounts for the few texts he leaves us, and for
the additional fact that he had no real chance to author systematic
works of the sort that Thomas Aquinas left behind. The works which
have come down to us today include several versions of his
Commentary on the *Sentences*, a major source work for medieval
thinkers. Each student was required to lecture on Peter Lombard's
Sentences during his years of bachelor study. The *Sentences* deals with all
major areas of knowledge about God, the world and human destiny. We
have two main versions of Scotus's lectures on this text, the *Lectura* (an
early commentary) and the *Ordinatio*.[2] Before his death, Scotus had
begun to prepare his definitive version and this is entitled *Ordinatio*,
because he revised some questions and corrected others. This work is
the main source for Scotus's mature insights, although sometimes reference to the *Lectura* text can be enlightening. In addition to his work on
the *Sentences*, Scotus also participated in public debates, called
Quodlibetal Questions.[3] His major metaphysical work on the existence of
God, *On the First Principle (De Primo Principio)*, provides the framework
for his philosophical perspective. Finally, Scotus authored several com-

---

[2]   The critical, or Vatican edition, was begin in 1951 under the direction of the
late Charles Balic. At this time only Books I and II of the *Lectura* and *Ordinatio*
versions have appeared.

[3]   Felix Alluntis and Allan Wolter, OFM published an English version of these
in *God and Creatures: The Quodlibetal Questions*, Princeton University Press
1975.

mentaries on various works of Aristotle, of which the *Subtle Questions on the Metaphysics* are the most important for us. In addition, Allan B. Wolter, OFM has undertaken to publish translations of texts he has established over his years of research and teaching. In *Duns Scotus on the Will and Morality*[4] he presents texts related to Scotus's moral theory. In *Duns Scotus's Early Oxford Lecture on Individuation*[5] we find the *Lectura* teaching on *haecceitas*, or the principle of individuation. Finally in *Duns Scotus's Political and Economic Philosophy*, Wolter presents texts from *Ordinatio* IV, distinction 15.[6] It should be clear from these titles that the thought of Scotus is still in process of discovery and study. Because the critical Vatican edition is not yet complete, contemporary scholars encounter Duns Scotus as a new thinker, emerging at long last from the shadow of Thomas Aquinas.

Scotus's movements early in his religious life may provide us with a clue about the dynamic philosophical milieu at the close of the 13th century. The entire century had been marked by the revolutionary entrance of Aristotle as a major philosophical voice in Western Europe. While the logical texts (*Organon*) had been translated into Latin by Boethius in the 6th century, it was only in the 12th that his major works (*Metaphysics, De Anima*) appeared in Latin. These were translated in portions by scholars in Toledo, and were received in installments in the universities of Western Europe. By 1260, the Latin universities had acquired all works of the Aristotelian corpus, including *Nicomachean Ethics* and *Politics.*[7]

As one might imagine, the integration of Aristotelian philosophy into Christianity was not an easy matter. In fact, the mid-13th century was a period of intense philosophical discussion between the Faculty of Theology and the Faculty of Arts at the Universities of Paris and Oxford. Study of Aristotle was not favorably received by theologians, particularly as it produced Masters of Arts who relied entirely upon the Aristotelian view of reality for their teaching. As early as 1215, public lectures on the *Metaphysics* and *De Anima* were forbidden. This prohibi-

---

[4]   Catholic University of America Press 1986.
[5]   Santa Barbara CA, Old Mission 1992.
[6]   Santa Barbara CA, Old Mission 1989.
[7]   For the chronology of the entrance of these texts, see Bernard G. Dod, "Aristoteles Latinus" in *The Cambridge History of Later Medieval Philosophy*, Kretzmann, Kenny, Pinborg (ed.), Cambridge University Press 1982, 45-79.

tion was repeated in 1245, apparently to no avail, for a new group of "lay scholars" was emerging in the schools. These men were not clerics, nor did they teach theology. Rather, they saw philosophy as the highest science and devoted their lives to the study of the Philosopher, Aristotle, and to the Commentator, Averroes. For this reason, they came to be known as "Averroists." Scholars today refer to them as "radical or integrist Aristotelians": masters who study Aristotle the way theologians study Scripture.

The rise of these "radical" philosophers did not go unnoticed by the theologians and ecclesiastical hierarchy. In Paris, for example, there were no less than five major condemnations of Aristotle's teachings on the soul and on the possibility of true human happiness in this life. Despite these attempts to restrict teaching and public discussion of Aristotle in 1215, 1245, 1260 and most notably 1277, professors and students alike continued to study and discuss the insights of this important Greek philosopher. Even Thomas Aquinas, with his sympathetic reading of Aristotle, did not escape posthumous condemnation in 1277 (Paris) and again in 1284 (Oxford).

Of all the censures, the Condemnation of 1277 figures as the most important. On March 7, 1277 no fewer than 219 propositions were condemned by Stephen Tempier, Bishop of Paris. Among these propositions were teachings of some Parisian Masters: teachings taken from Averroes and Aristotle which claimed that a life devoted to philosophy was superior to the life of faith, that there is only one Mind for all humanity (Monopsychism), that the movement of the stars determine human action (astral determinism) and that the will must choose what the intellect dictates. The condemnation was repeated in 1284 in Oxford. The final years of the 13th century saw an increased amount of debate and discussion over the possibility of a dialogue between Aristotelian philosophy and Christianity.

As we concentrate on the ethical elements of Scotus's thinking in later chapters, we must not neglect the way he goes about doing philosophy. A desire for mutuality with other traditions reveals itself in his intellectual honesty and openness to other positions. In fact, his concern for the other side of any discussion is so great, that he often loses the reader in his presentation of his opponent's viewpoint. Many scholars say that Scotus gives a better presentation of the other viewpoint than does the opponent himself. He takes great pains to defend another's position with the best arguments available and he answers these arguments methodically. This type of openness is rare in any thinker, and all the more surprising when one is dealing with a non-Christian opponent. In some cases, he offers several acceptable positions, each with its own strengths, before declaring his own preference. In his writing style Scotus shows himself to be open to new ideas, ready to hear convincing arguments, but just as ready to think things out for himself and evaluate each position from a Christian perspective.

Finally, a word about the title. I have chosen to present Scotus's moral perspective not as a defense of the primacy of freedom in moral living, but rather as an appeal for the harmony of goodness and as an expression of mutuality at all levels of human living. Mutuality entails reciprocity and produces communion. As a dimension internal to the moral person, mutuality appears as a *balance* between moral affections or dispositions. This balance produces peace within the moral agent. Externally, mutuality expresses goodness as *harmony* among several aspects surrounding the morally good act. Together, internal balance and external harmony unite in the fulfillment of human living. Their communion forms a dynamic whole which reaches out toward God in friendship and love. The entire journey of human living, from internal choices to external actions, culminates in mutuality with God and with all persons.

one

A Structure for Mutuality

Any discussion of Scotist ethical insights must take into account the stereotype of this Franciscan which exists in the minds of many students of history. It is true that Scotus is often judged against the imposing figure of Thomas Aquinas and found wanting. Aquinas has provided Western thought with one of the most compelling ethical visions within Christianity. Huge portions of his *Summa Theologiae* are devoted to an intricate examination of happiness, natural virtue, moral law and rational moral judgment. Against this Dominican vision, Scotus often appears to defend an arbitrary moral universe, dependent upon the whim of a divine lawgiver. The centrality of freedom in Scotist thought is often portrayed as devoid of rationality. The God of Scotus seems too unpredictable. Some of this misunderstanding is due to the fragmented and sparse treatment of ethical issues found in Scotist texts. True enough, it is not possible to discover a full-blown ethical theory or procedure which we might attribute to Duns Scotus.

However, when we consider the importance of freedom for modern thought, it would be misguided to dismiss Scotus as an insignificant contributor to moral discussion. His is a vision of reality which emphasizes the value of each individual being as a concrete manifestation of divine love and creativity. Scotus's attention to the value of the contingent reveals his deeper concern to defend divine initiative operative in history. His focus on the "thisness" of each thing points to the value of creation precisely as willed by God.

The connection he draws between contingency and freedom does

1

not remain within the domain of divine activity: it grounds his discussion of the value of moral living as a process of transformation and participation in divine life. In other words, the structure of Scotist thought moves from an awareness of the value and beauty of creation to the affirmation that such beauty could only be the result of a free and rational act. Once he has described the sort of freedom necessary in God, he concludes that moral living involves human imitation of divine perfection: the fullness of freedom is creativity in love. This perfection is ultimately creative of relationship, just as all reality forms a whole, just as the Covenant with Abraham established a friendship between God and Israel, just as the Incarnation reveals a divine-human union, so too the goal of human moral living is the creation of a moral community and participation in the Trinitarian communion.

These important threads are woven together in Scotist thought: they form a dense fabric which is difficult to analyze. In addition, the close relationship between philosophy and theology for medieval thinkers influences the way in which human and divine realities overlap in Scotist texts. Because he sees the human journey as revealing divine activity, Scotus accepts that any discussion of the human person reveals something about divine nature and, conversely, that any discussion of God points out a potential perfectibility within human life. So it is not surprising to find that his discussion of freedom moves easily between the consideration of human freedom and of its basis in divine activity.

In 1990, Marilyn McCord Adams edited a collection of articles written by Allan B. Wolter, OFM entitled *The Philosophical Theology of John Duns Scotus*.[1] This title is an especially apt description of the overall nature of Scotus's work: philosophical theology. As was the case for many medieval thinkers, Scotus viewed philosophy and theology as collaborative sciences: reason and faith are not at odds. The two disciplines seek to explain, each in its own way and from its own point of view (Scotus would say "its own formal object"), the intricate mystery of reality. This mystery includes both the naturally knowable and the revealed. For this reason, Scotus opens his *Sentence* Commentary with a Prologue in which he defends the "necessity of revealed doctrine" for a proper

---

[1]   Cornell University Press.

understanding of what it means to be human.[2] His analysis considers reality according to a double axis: conscious of the limitations of human cognition and in light of the importance of divine freedom.

In the Prologue, Scotus clearly sets forth his philosophical-theological perspective. This perspective involves the central intuition about the limits of human understanding and, consequently, the need for divine assistance. No discussion of human nature, human fulfillment, the present condition of human life after the Fall,[3] or the limitations of human understanding appears without an allusion to divine grace and the importance of revelation. For Scotus, the discussion of human reality always unfolds to reveal a discussion of the human-divine: the human which we know and the divine to which we aspire.

In this first chapter, I present significant elements from Scotus's philosophical and theological vision. These elements correspond to the overall context of the wind chime; they define its form. In addition, they offer a structure from which a better understanding of his ethical insights may emerge. The elements themselves come from theological, metaphysical and epistemological domains. They all focus on a central commitment to the value of freedom and the contingent. Scotus rejects the necessitarian universe defended by the Arab philosophers whose commentaries accompanied the translation of Aristotelian texts during the 13th century. Through this rejection of determinism, his teaching presents a clear and strong defense of divine freedom for creation of this world and of the beings which inhabit it. As later chapters make clear, the value of the particular and concrete within creation is an important foundation for Scotus's ethical insights.

I choose to begin with a vision of the whole: a discussion of the spiritual tradition within which Scotus lived and a presentation of the divine nature as Triune communion. These two aspects reflect the intimate relationship between human and divine realities. The human person is image of God (*imago Dei*), created with the potential to participate in divine life. The Trinity manifests that life in a communion of persons. As such, it represents the exemplar for human society.

Following this, I present the value of creation and the contingent particular through Scotus's theories of *haecceitas* (thisness), of abstractive

---

[2]   Vatican 1:1-58. There are two editions which are used in Scotist study. The older Vivès edition will always be indicated in parentheses. No indication of edition refers to the critical Vatican publication.

[3]   Scotus refers to this condition as *pro statu isto*, or in the present state.

and intuitive cognitional acts and of the essential order within reality. Finally, we conclude with the order of freedom as ground for the moral order. In particular, this is found in Scotus's position on the Incarnation as free manifestation of divine liberality, not as consequence of original sin. Divine freedom is also made manifest in the order of merit, or God's free acceptance to reward human actions far beyond what they deserve.

The purpose of this chapter is to map out the moral domain and to highlight the originality of Scotus's vision. This domain is Christocentric: it does not focus on human sinfulness. It is a vision of divine creativity and liberality, rather than divine justice. It is a vision of creation, of the present moment as holding the key to an encounter with God: an incarnational moral discussion. This means that, for Scotus, to speak of things human is to enter the domain of divinity. No human action is trivial, no human decision unimportant. The moral order extends to and unifies an entire life. It is not limited to a narrow set of cases for moral decisions. Moral living does not involve problem solving alone: it is the rational manifestation of divine life within an order of right loving.

The Spiritual Tradition

Scotus writes within a tradition which might be called *wisdom spirituality*. According to this spiritual tradition, the human person is identified as image of God (*imago Dei*) on a journey toward more complete resemblance to God. The moral journey imitates divine activity in free creativity. A proper notion of God, then, is necessary background to any discussion of moral living or rationality. This spiritual tradition originated in Eastern Christianity, with writers such as Irenaeus, Origen and Gregory of Nyssa. For these early Eastern and mystical writers, human life unfolds as a process of divinization begun and completed by God through the action of divine grace. At its earliest beginnings in the East, this tradition emphasized divine and not human agency.

Key ideas and insights from the East were transmitted to the Latin West via homilies; their spiritual insights formed a common patrimony for the early Church. For scholars like Augustine the *imago Dei* or "image of God" phrase in the Genesis creation story became the source for reflection upon reasoning and willing in the dynamic process of purification and divinization. Augustine's work was seminal for the development of psychological and moral aspects of the *imago Dei* tradition viewed as a spiritual process or journey toward God. In the West, this developed into a tradition which was much more practical and less mystical than its Eastern counterpart, since it focused on personal response rather than on divine activity in human transformation.

Augustine identifies God's image in us as the highest dimension of our soul: the mind (*mens, intellectus*) which is the "interior and intelligible eye."[4] In his *De Trinitate*, the mind, with its faculties and activities, is the image of the entire Trinity. The process of conversion and reformation takes place within a precise relationship to the second person of the Trinity as Word (*Verbum*), by whom the mind is joined to the source of being (*Principium*) and the source of goodness (*Spiritus*).

The Augustinian tradition holds the key to any discussion of human dignity; each person is the image of God. In addition, these insights provide the foundation for a reflection upon the process of divinization as growth in resemblance to God. Transformation into God constitutes the goal of all human living. The image of God within each person becomes the resemblance of God that we are meant to be. This resemblance is lost through original sin, but can be regained through baptism and the life of grace. Thus the human capacity for God (*imago*) is meant for the fullness of union with and possession of God, thanks to the workings of grace: divine love in the soul. Augustine offers a systematic presentation of what it means to be human, both as a metaphysical reality (the way we are) and as a dynamic spirituality which points beyond itself toward life with God (what we are meant to be).

The reality of sin, and particularly the moral weakness caused by original sin, takes its place in this overall vision of the human journey. Augustine's position on original sin has had a particular influence on Latin Christianity. Writers of the Middle Ages sought to account for the possibility of sin, and particularly sin in light of knowledge, such as Adam and Eve must have enjoyed in the Garden of Eden. As the Franciscans develop their own response to this question, they emphasize the ability of the will to make choices, even those which may run counter to good judgment.

The dual threads of capacity for God and the effects of original sin entwine to form the fabric of medieval moral discussion. On the one hand, the *imago Dei* notion of divine life within us informs our actions with God's grace. On the other hand, the negative consequences of the

---

[4] On Diverse Questions 83, 46,2 and 51,1 in Migne, PL 40, 30b and 32 ab.

Fall offset any optimism about human motivation. This internal tension between human aspiration and moral performance forms the context for the 13th century discussion of true human fulfillment and its relationship to this life.

But the 12th century renaissance also contributed another dimension to the moral discussion: the cosmic participation of all nature. In the 11th and 12th centuries, the school of St. Victor (Victorines) and the Cistercians enhanced the Platonic aspects of the Augustinian dynamic and linked the human journey toward God with the movement of all reality in a giant cosmic return. Richard of St. Victor (✠ 1173) identified creation as *imago Dei* and made use of the microcosm/macrocosm analogy to point out how all reality "trembles with dynamism" in its movement toward God. As the human soul animates the body, so too the world soul animates the cosmos. Both human and cosmic reality are on a journey which will only reach culmination at the end of time. And, while the cosmic journey is a natural one, the human journey depends upon the free choice to return to God.

Augustinian echoes were present in this cosmic return. The Cistercian tradition dealt with the dynamic human journey precisely as a tension between the image (as capacity for God in liberty) and resemblance (as satisfaction found in union with God). This tension could only be resolved with divine aid. The source of the tension was localized in the imperfection inherent in human loving, a disorder resulting from original sin. Thus, the first step within the process of transfiguration into resemblance to God begins with right and ordered loving. For William of St. Thierry, the goal of each person unites all persons and all creation with and in God. What might have developed into an individual moral endeavor was contextualized within this cosmic spiritual journey, thanks to the insights of the 12th century theologians. There is no merely personal salvation: all creation groans and trembles as it gives birth to the Reign of God. The dynamic spirituality of 12th century thinkers promoted the return of all reality (human and natural) to God, even in light of human weakness.

The Franciscans of the 13th century sought to enhance the influences of the Augustinian tradition and of 12th century Platonic spirituality. Their contribution identified *imago Dei* with the structure of the human soul. We are God's image because our soul is one in essence, yet with three powers: memory, understanding and will. For Alexander of Hales and John of la Rochelle, the first real philosophers within the

Franciscan tradition, the divine image unites both the cognitive (head) and affective (heart) domains. There is, in fact, a double trinity: in the domain of knowledge it is mind, intellect and will; in the realm of action it is free choice, reason and willing. While the cognitive domain gives rise to the image, it is the activity of loving which demonstrates resemblance and, therefore, divinization. Thus, the Franciscan tradition saw the image of God within the soul as exhibiting a spiritual dynamism involving acts of knowing and loving. In addition, all Franciscan writers emphasized the superiority of loving over knowing, since it is by the act of love that we most resemble God's gracious activity. While knowing provides the image, loving transforms us into the resemblance of God. Moral life, then, is that process of divinization by which we imitate divine life.

More than any other Franciscan thinker, Bonaventure (✠1274) overtly linked systematic and spiritual theology, speculation and mysticism. For him, the *imago Dei* doctrine became a philosophy of life. Utilizing both Augustinian trinitarian analysis and the development of John of la Rochelle, Bonaventure presented *imago* as belonging to our natural gifts and resemblance (*similitudo*) as the result of the gifts of grace. "Image as to nature, resemblance as to grace" is a formula from Alexander and John's *Summa* which appeared in other texts of the same tradition. In both his *Breviloquium* and *Retracing of the Arts to Theology*, Bonaventure uses the term *imago* to refer to the capacity for knowledge of God. Resemblance or *similitudo* refers, rather, to the indwelling of God. The entire journey from image to resemblance is found clearly presented in the classic Bonaventurian text, *The Mind's Road to God*. Here contemplation of God by and in the vestiges found in creation and the images within the soul (both natural and reformed by grace) ultimately raises the soul beyond itself by resemblance to divine light and "in this light itself."[5] Central to Bonaventure's thought, *imago Dei* is perhaps the most important aspect of his spirituality and anthropology. The human person is defined primarily in relationship to God, a relationship of dependence which includes gratitude, knowledge and love.

The *imago Dei* motif is an important one for Scotus as well, yet he is quick to note the limitations of human self-awareness. In Quodlibet 14 he states that the image of God within the human soul is not naturally knowable, due to the limitations of human cognition. We can, he

---

[5]   Bonaventure, *The Mind's Road to God*, VII, 1, Liberal Arts Press 1953, p. 43.

affirms, know that our source is God and still not understand the exact relationship which exists between Creator and image. This relationship is unknowable because, in order to understand any relationship, we must understand both terms. In the case of our nature as image of God, we fail to grasp God's nature as infinite being, and therefore are unable to conceive of ourselves "for the absolute things that we are." We know something about who we are, but we cannot fathom on our own what God is really like.

> Consequently, even though the foundation can be known natural-
> ly by such a knower, it does not follow that he can know the rela-
> tion naturally....an entity which is essentially a relationship to
> something unlimited, even though it be limited in itself, is to the
> created intellect no more intelligible naturally than is the [infinite]
> term without which the relationship itself is unthinkable.[6]

It is not that we cannot know ourselves, rather we cannot grasp the relationship we have to God in the absence of some revelation such as the account of creation in Genesis 1. While philosophy is capable of dealing with the metaphysical dimensions of relationship, such as the univocity of being and essential order, these insights do not exhaust the relationship to God which theology is capable of knowing through Scripture. Philosophy may deal adequately with the dependency of created being on a First Principle. Theology alone is able to discover the triune communion which constitutes divine nature. For the Christian, it is the triune character of God as imaged in the human person which takes on significance for the moral journey. There is obviously a significant difference between God understood as Unmoved Mover and as a Trinity of Persons sharing life. For Scotus, the goal of the moral journey is transformation into divine life. This goal cannot be understood apart from reflection upon the nature of a triune God.

The Trinity: Persons in Communion

Scotus's discussion of the Trinity is significant in light of the two traditional strains, coming from Eastern and Western thought, which deal with the unity of nature and Trinity of Persons in God. Eastern thinkers emphasized that divine unity has its source in the Father as

[6]   Quodlibet 14, nn. 23-4, 14.83-4 in Alluntis/Wolter *God and Creatures: The Quodlibetal Questions*, p. 339.

Source of Being. The Latin tradition appealed to the Holy Spirit as *nexus amoris* (loving bond) between Father and Son. This difference of emphasis on the principle for communion within God, either as source or as bond of love, lay at the heart of what was to become the *Filioque* controversy at the Council of Lyons in 1274. How one understands the Holy Spirit determines whether one speaks of spiration from the Father alone or from the Father and the Son.

This section involves the most technical and specialized presentation of the book. It is of such importance that I cannot avoid a discussion appropriate to the issue. It constitutes the key insight to the value of mutuality, the communion of shared life among persons. In the Trinity exists both unity and communion, God is One and Three. At an early period of his teaching, Scotus held that personhood is constituted not by relationship, but by something absolute. This absolute is explained by means of logical and metaphysical terminology proper to scholastic discussion.

While Scotus does not alter the traditional Latin approach and accepts the Augustinian trinitarian psychology, he leans toward a more Eastern understanding of the Trinity.[7] Scotus asserts that the essence of God involves both an incommunicable dimension proper to each Person and a communal dimension which can only be described within a relationship. The dimension is incommunicable because it lies beyond language. It is expressed through language but is not itself reducible to the terms which are used to describe it. Scotus calls this the logical *suppositum* (term) which is necessary prior to any discussion of relationship. The relational language of paternity and generation refer to personal properties which can only be grasped for one person in terms of another.

As the editors of the critical edition note, Scotus's early teaching in Oxford defended the absolute constitution of the Father in the Trinity, in the absence of any discussion of relationship among the persons. Each person in the Trinity is a person in an absolute sense (*per modos essendi*) and not relative to the others (*per relationes*). As this position ran counter to the traditional Augustinian position found in the *De Trinitate*, Scotus was forced to revoke his early teaching to accept the common opinion.[8] The fact that Scotus had to adjust his teaching to

---

[7]   On this, see Reinhold Oswald Messner "Die Ökumenische Bedeutung der Skotischen Trinitätslehre" *De Doctrina I. Duns Scoti* III, 653-726.

[8]   *Liber propugnatorius* quoted in Vatican 6:1*.

accommodate the more traditional, relational teaching gives evidence of his desire to defend both the existence of personal and communal dimensions and the dynamic essence which is the fruit of this communion.

In his discussion of the constitution of the divine persons in *Lectura* I, 26, Scotus favors the position which argues for some sort of absolute constitutive cause for each person in the Trinity. This position, he states, is not contrary to the faith and is more probable than the traditional argument for personhood as relationship taken from Augustine's *De Trinitate.*

> Holding this position, it must be said that persons are not constituted by relationships, but by something absolute; and so three persons in God are primarily absolute, however followed by relations to which they are referred.[9]

We see in this early formulation that Scotus holds both person and communion as essential to divine life. He offers a basis for the relationship among persons which, he asserts, constitutes the personality but not the metaphysical *suppositum* (basis) for the relationship. In other words, personality is the result of relationship. I am who I am by virtue of my relationships to others throughout my life. But description of my personality does not exhaust the mystery of my personhood. The deeper mystery of each individual is ineffable, and only finds expression in relationship. The possibility of relationship depends upon the existence of persons who are capable of being related. No relationship can exist where there are not two terms which are joined together.

The discussion from the Quodlibetal Questions clarifies this insight relative to the essence of God as Triune communion. Scotus states in Quodlibet 1 that God's essence is incommunicable and can be conceived as different from the relationships among the three persons:

> For he is truly unique, because incommunicable and he revealed this as his name to Moses his servant when he said: "I am who am." But whether one uses essence, speaking properly or substance speaking improperly, both are affirmed of what he is in himself and not of what he is in relationship to something.[10]

---

[9]   N. 54 (17:332).
[10]   Quodl. 1, n. 3, 1.5–1.6, *God and Creatures,* pp. 6-7.

As Scotus continues he explains that the substance of the Father is the Father himself, not insofar as he is Father, but insofar as he is. In Quodlibet 4, his point is clarified logically in terms of the word "subsist." In one sense it refers to the essence of God as a *per se* unity, but in another sense it refers to each person who possesses being "incommunicably."

> In this sense there are three "subsistents," since there are three persons or personalities, for there are three incommunicable subsistents, even though there is but one per se being.[11]

At this point, Scotus enhances the logical analysis with a theological insight. God's essence is communion, for the theological meaning of the term *essential* refers not to the logical or metaphysical suppositum necessary for a predicable statement (which is commonly opposed to the term *accidental*[12]), but rather as opposed to the term *notional* and refers to the real community among all three persons:

> On the other hand, the theologians apply the term essential to the divine in a different sense [from the philosophers]. The essence, being the absolutely first, as has been said, is common with real community to all three persons alike, for it is affirmed singularly of each person as well as of all three together. For this reason, then, anything else predicated similarly in the divine is called essential, because it is similar to the essence in the mode of predication or in community.[13]

It is significant to consider that, in the above discussion, Scotus brings together the domains of language (logic), metaphysics and theology to unpack the intricate mystery of a Triune God. Here is an excellent example of the philosopher-theologian at work.

In *Ordinatio* I, 26, Scotus emphasizes that the divine persons cannot be understood in abstraction from their communal relationship. In his defense of the position for the absolute constitutive entity in each person, Scotus affirms that it is not contrary to the faith, if one remembers that the essence of God must always be described in terms such that the human intellect can grasp, however vaguely, something about God.

---

[11] Quodl. 4, n. 20, 4.46, *God and Creatures*, p. 98.

[12] "Essential, therefore, signifies in philosophy that which is included per se in the essence." (Quodl. 1, n. 5, 1.13, *God and Creatures*, p. 9).

[13] Quodl. 1, n. 5, 1.14, *God and Creatures*, pp. 9-10.

Thus, Jesus described the relations within God in terms which could be understood by us. This position does not defend absolute distinctions among the persons such that the essence is difference, but only refers to the reality of the person *secundo modo.*[14] He concludes that the position for absolute constitution is not contrary to the faith and any difficulties can indeed be resolved, even if the position for relations be true.[15]

Scotus's discussion of the relations among Persons in the Trinity is significant for several reasons. First, it affirms the individual personhood of each member of the Trinity as a suppositum for divine relationship. Second, this individuality provides the metaphysical basis for the relationship of triune communion. Anything theology says about God as Trinity requires relational language. Thus, a relationship of communion characterizes divine life and surpasses whatever distinctions among persons the human mind might conceive. Third, the Trinity is a communion of persons exemplifying the goal of all human activity. Union with another or others out of love is the key to human fulfillment because this union is generative and life-giving. In its fullness, the human experience of relationship and mutuality images divine life.

This is a key insight to the importance of mutuality for Scotus. No descriptive relationship exhausts the substantial identity of anyone or anything. However, neither does any person or any being exist outside of relationship with others. Thus, while we can conceive of the essence of the Father independently of the Son or Spirit, we cannot speak of the First Person of the Trinity in any way without reference to the relationship with the others. At a fundamental level, all substances are individual and distinct. In the dynamic whole, they all function in relationship: some through mutuality and self-gift. The mystery of all reality can be summarized as "individuals in relationship."

The Value of Contingent Reality

A striking feature of Scotist thought is the importance he places upon the individuality of each creature. Indeed, this aspect of his thinking greatly influenced the 19th century Jesuit, Gerard Manley Hopkins, who dubbed Scotus "of realty [*sic*] the rarest-veined unraveller" ("Duns Scotus' Oxford"). Scotus's emphasis upon the importance of individual-

[14]   N. 59 (6:24).
[15]   N. 93 (6:49). The editors refer the reader to *Lectura* I, 26, n. 75 (17:340).

ity appears clearly in his notion of *haecceitas* (thisness) which makes each person as well as each object an irreplaceable piece of the glorious whole which is creation. The determining factor of *haecceity* is that it is the ineffable in each being, the "ultimate reality of being"[16] which can only be described, never exhausted, by language.

The Latin term *haecceitas* appears only twice in Scotus's discussion of individuation, in his *Reportatio* Book II, D. 3[17] and in his *Subtle Questions on Aristotle's Metaphysics*. In this latter work Scotus defines the principle of individuation as follows: "I say briefly that any form of which there is any sort of species is composed of some potency and act, and every one is a "this" [*haec*] by means of an individual form."[18]

Scotus argues that the principle of individuation must be intrinsic, unique and proper to each individual.[19] It must be a positive entity which is incapable of reproduction: the undivided individual of each being.[20] The thisness (*haecceitas*) which differentiates one person from another can only be known by a direct acquaintance, and not from any consideration of any "common nature." Thus, *haecceitas* makes a singular thing what it is and differentiates it from all other things (of a common nature) to which it may be compared (because of the commonality). *Haecceitas* "contracts the indifference of the specific nature to just one unique individual."[21]

This *haec* or ultimate principle of reality cannot be known *per se* by our intellect. Scotus admits that in this life only what can be abstracted from sense perception motivates the intellect. But this does not exclude the possibility of an intellect strong enough to have a direct intellection of the *haecceitas*, such as the divine or an angelic act of intellection. *Haecceitas* is intelligible, even though we are not capable of such intellection in this life. To make this point, Scotus cites Aristotle: "As the eyes of the owl are to the blazing sun, so is the reason in our soul to the things which are by nature most evident of all" (*Metaphysics* II, ch. 1, 993b9-11).

---

16   *Ordinatio* II, 3, q. 6 n. 188 (7:483).

17   At nn. 25, 29, 31 and 32.

18   In *QQ Meta.* VII, q. 13 (Vivès 7:416b). On the use of the term *haecceitas* see Wolter, "Scotus' Individuation Theory" in *Philosophical Theology*, note 26, p. 76.

19   II, 3, n. 164 in *Duns Scotus' Early Oxford Lecture on Individuation*, Old Mission: Santa Barbara 1992, p. 80.

20   "what cannot be cloned" according to Wolter, ibid. p. 73.

21   Wolter, "Scotus' Individuation Theory" in *Philosophical Theology*, p. 90.

Haecceitas refers to that positive dimension of every concrete and contingent being which identifies it and makes it worthy of attention. At the close of the 13th century, Scotus shifts from a focus on the necessary and universal toward the particular: this shift was decisive. As a philosophical term of individuation, *haecceitas* enabled Scotus to emphasize the ineffable value of each contingent being and, indirectly, the enormous liberality of God who created this *haec* out of numerous possibilities. *Haecceitas* is a central insight into a vision of reality in which freedom functions as primary cause. Without denying the scientific value of the necessary and universal, Scotus expands the domain of rational reflection to include contingent reality and thus make room for theology as a science which considers not only the nature of God (as a necessary being) but also the actions of God in human history, actions which are recounted in scripture. Theology is not merely a speculative science in the Aristotelian sense, but a practical science (*praxis*) which deals with human reflection upon revelation understood as contingent acts of divine generosity and liberality within human history.

Scotus extends the value of the contingent and particular to philosophical reflection as well. Following Aristotle, he affirms that metaphysical reflection begins with contingent experience. In the first lines of the *Ordinatio* we read that the natural object of human understanding is *ens inquantum ens,* or any contingent being insofar as it is or exists: "But the first object of our natural intellect is any being in so far as it is [*ens inquantum ens*]." [22] The link between being and cognition results in what scholars call the "moderate Realism" of Scotist thought which accepts some sort of isomorphism between concepts and reality. As the object of intellection, *ens* cannot be discussed in abstraction from the sorts of cognitive acts of which the mind is capable. Because of the intimate relation between being and knowing, Allan Wolter places his discussion of Scotus's theory of individuation in light of his cognitive theories. [23]

The rich and intricate relations among concepts and with extramental reality is understood by means of the cognitive act of abstraction or generalization. The experience of an actually existing extramental individual gives rise to a cognitive apprehension of the more general concepts of "individual nature" and "common nature."

[22] *Ordinatio* Prologue, Pars Prima, unica, n. 1 (1:2.).
[23] Wolter, "Scotus' Individuation Theory", p. 71.

Individual natures are real, extramental substantial entities with a corresponding *per se* unity.[24] Common natures are conceptually indistinguishable but individually instantiated. Thus, "humanity" would be an example of a common nature, that is, common to all human beings, while *Socrateity* would be an instance of an individual nature which is only found in this particular individual, Socrates. Knowing *Socrateity* is only possible through a knowledge of the actually existing Socrates, and is itself a cognitive act which is already once removed from the direct experience of the concrete individual.

In addition to the cognitive capacity for abstraction, Scotus claims a more direct access to reality on the part of the mind: intuition. In *Ordinatio* II, 3, he identifies the difference between abstractive and intuitive acts. "I may speak briefly, I call knowledge of the quiddity itself *abstractive* ... [and] that of a thing according to its actual existence or of a thing present in its existence I call *intuitive intellection.*"[25] Intuition is a direct vision (*visio*)[26] of an actually existing object as existing. Quodlibet 14 clarifies that intuition is possible due to the presence of the object "in all its proper intelligibility" and not via a mental representation:

> Any such intellection, namely, that which is per se, proper, and immediate, requires the presence of the object in all its proper intelligibility as object [*propria ratio objecti*]. If the intellection is intuitive, this means in its own existence it is present as object. If the intellection is abstractive, it is present in something which represents it in all its proper and essential meaning as a knowable object.[27]

In the *De Primo Principio* intuitive cognition is deemed superior to abstractive, by virtue of the fact that it is immediate knowledge and does not depend upon a mental image or phantasm:

> Knowledge through what is similar is merely knowledge under a universal aspect, to the extent that the things are alike. Through such a universal what properly distinguishes each would remain unknown. Furthermore, such a knowledge through a universal is

---

[24] See Wolter's discussion of this in *Early Oxford Lecture...*, p. xiii.
[25] *Ordinatio* II, 3, q. 2, n. 321 (7:553).
[26] Quodl. 7 n. 8 in *God and Creatures* 7.21, pp. 166-7.
[27] Quodl. 14, n. 10 in *God and Creatures* 14.36, p. 325.

not intuitive but abstractive, and intuitive knowledge is the more perfect of the two.[28]

While abstract knowledge is proper to scientific reflection, particularly in the Aristotelian sense, intuitive cognition reaches the object precisely in itself and in the act of existence.[29] Thus, while abstractive cognition can occur with an existing as well as a non-existing object, intuitive cognition can only occur with an existing object.[30]

Scotus asserts that the theologian would in fact have a better assessment of human cognitive acts than would the philosopher, since the latter is only aware of his actual experience of cognition.[31] The theologian can account for more powerful cognitive acts, based upon the insight from Scripture that, after the Fall, the human condition is distinct from human nature.[32] Along with Bonaventure and other members of the Augustinian tradition, Scotus agrees that, in this life, the effects of original sin are such that cognition is impaired.

---

[28] *A Treatise on God*, p. 149.

[29] "What distinguishes intuitive cognition from any other kind of knowledge is the fact that it gives us knowledge of an existent as existing." Sebastian Day, *Intuitive Cognition: a Key to the Later Scholastics*, Franciscan Institute Press 1957, p. 82. Richard Dumont identifies here the key difference between Scotist and Kantian epistemologies: "The crucial difference between the Kantian and Scotistic noetic is the issue of intellectual intuition. Whereas Kant simply denies to the human intellect an intuitive access to reality, Scotus does not." "Intuition: Prescript or Postscript to Scotus' Demonstration of God's Existence" in *Deus et Homo ad mentem I. Duns Scoti*, Rome 1972, p. 86.

[30] Quodl. 7 n. 8, *God and Creatures* 7.22, p. 167.

[31] "The Philosopher, however, would say this present state is simply natural to man, having experienced no other and having no cogent reason for concluding another state exists. He perhaps would go on to claim that the adequate object of the human intellect, even by its nature as a power, is simply what he perceived to be commensurate to it at present, [i.e., the quiddity of sensible things]." Quodl. 14, n. 12, *God and Creatures* 14.45, p. 327. See also *Ordinatio* I, 3, nn. 115, 123-4 (3: 71-2, 76-7).

[32] "This at least is what would have to be admitted by a theologian who claims our present state is not natural and that our impotence in regard to many intelligible matters represents a penal, not a natural situation, according to [Augustine] in *De Trinitate* 'Things that are certain are revealed to your interior eyes by that light', namely that eternal light of which he has spoken. 'What is the reason, then, why you are unable to see it with a steady gaze except indeed your infirmity; and what has brought this upon you except sin?'" *God and Creatures* 14.44, p. 327.

Scotus's focus upon the concrete particular is the basis for his discussion of metaphysics and theology as sciences. Metaphysical reflection is attention to the conceptual framework which grounds concrete experience. Theology deals with the contingent experiences of God revealed in Scripture. Scotus's commitment to actually existing concrete reality grounds his metaphysics on human experience and establishes the Aristotelian dimension of his thought. Wolfgang Kluxen places special emphasis upon this aspect of Scotist thought, and especially notes that Scotist metaphysics is not the establishment of a separate realm of ideas.[33] Paul Vignaux points to the important insights surrounding the notion of being particularly as it relates to the opening prayer of the *De Primo Principio*, where Scotus appeals to the divine act of self-revelation to Moses as "I am who am." Reflection upon the concept *ens* provides a rational basis for a demonstration of God's existence precisely because God has chosen *being* as an appropriate description of his essence as it can be known by the human intellect.[34]

Both Kluxen and Vignaux support the point made by Wolter mentioned earlier, that is, that no discussion of metaphysics is possible without a discussion of cognition and, further, that to discuss metaphysics is in fact to discuss human intellection and the degree to which knowing and being are related. This isomorphism between being and knowing is an essential aspect of Scotist thinking and explains how the mind is able to move from the concrete particular of which *haecceitas* is the individuating principle to an understanding of the deeper relationships existing among natures and essences in reality.

At the ontological level of beings, this relatedness has a specific title: the essential order. This refers to the "order of essences" in reality, an order which involves relationship between prior and posterior. It is an order which joins all reality together and to God as First Cause.

> I do not take essential order, however, in the strict sense as do some who say that what is posterior is ordered whereas what is first or prior transcends order. I understand it rather in its common meaning as a relation which can be affirmed equally (*relatio aequiparantiae dicta*) of the prior and posterior in regard to each other. In other

---

[33] "Welterfahrung und Gottesbeweis: eine Studie zum "Tractatus de Primo Principio" des Johannes Duns Scotus" in *Deus et homo ad mentem I. Duns Scoti Rome* 1972, p. 59.

[34] "Métaphysique de l'Exode, philosophie de la religion (A partir du *De Primo Principio* selon Duns Scot)." *Rivista di Filosofia neo-scolastica,* 70 (1978), p. 136.

words I consider prior and posterior to be an adequate division of
whatever is ordered, so that we may use the terms order and priority or posteriority interchangeably.[35]

Thus, essential order means not only that creation is related to God, but
that God is related to creation. The essential order is a great sweep of
being, a unified whole of reality which includes God. As First Principle,
God does not exist outside the order of being nor outside of relationship with humanity.

The essential order is reflected in language we use. The term
"being," states Scotus, is univocal: it has only one meaning. This means
that we predicate being of God, of creatures, of the universe, and of the
person all in the same way: God is, the rocks are, I am. The verb "to be" in
each case is used in exactly the same way. This is the link of being which
founds the essential order. As First in the order of being, God is prior to
all other beings: God is Infinite Being. God's being is not, however,
beyond the realm of being, in the manner of the Neoplatonic One. We
do not leave being to encounter God; we encounter God in being, in
beings, in one another.

The relatedness of the essential order could be called a weak mutuality, since it is a relationship which can only be *predicated* equally of
each member of the order. It is not a mutuality which involves equality
of all members: creation and God are not equal, but they are both in
relationship. This weaker sense of mutuality appears at all levels of the
ontological spectrum: within nature, within the will, between the intellect and the will. In each case, one can predicate relationship of each
member, but the members are not equal. The will is, for Scotus, a superi-
or cause to the intellect. Freedom is a superior order to that of nature.
But the will and the intellect are in relationship to one another.
Freedom depends on nature for its exercise. All being is related, nothing exists on its own.

A stronger sense of mutuality emerges from a discussion of relationship among persons or between God and human persons. This
mutuality is stronger because it is based upon the free choice to enter
into relationship, to create relationship or to establish order. It depends
upon a free choice among persons to enter into relationship and ultimately communion. This communion appears in an exemplar manner
in the Trinity, a union among the persons which Scotus calls both neces-

---

[35]   In Wolter, *A Treatise on God*, 1.5, p. 2.

sary and free. It can also be seen in the divine initiative for the Covenant with Moses and the people of Israel, in the divine act of selflessness in the Incarnation and, finally, in the divine graciousness and liberality of *acceptatio* and the order of merit. The stronger meaning of mutuality as relatedness among persons is clearly a theological insight, for its understanding depends upon some reflection on Scripture: on the nature of God as Trinity, on the human person as created in God's image, on the person of Jesus Christ as Word-made-flesh and, finally, on the promise in Christ of an ultimate reward and union with God.

The Order of Freedom

The focus on contingent reality and upon the limitations proper to human cognition point to the deeper metaphysical basis for human experience. For Scotus, this basis is the order of freedom found in God. While within the Trinity the relationships among the persons are both necessary and free,[36] divine activity *ad extra* is a completely free act on the part of the divine will.[37] This order of freedom extends to creation and to the divine act of self-revelation to Moses: "I am who am" (Exodus 3:14). It is most complete, however, in the person of Jesus Christ.

The Incarnation is the central insight to Scotist moral thought. It most completely embodies the idea of divine freedom for self-revelation and relationship. Scotus places Jesus Christ, and not original sin, at the center of the moral discussion. In the person of Jesus both divine and human realities unite. Scotus's discussion of the reason for the Incarnation emphasizes divine freedom for self-revelation and relationship to humanity, without regard to human sinfulness. This is in sharp contrast to Anselm's classic argument in *Cur Deus Homo?*, where the Incarnation is tied to the "happy fault" of original sin. For Anselm, reparation for so heinous a crime could only be made by a person who was both human and divine. The Incarnation was explained in light of the Cross: the Passion and Death of Jesus. Scotus does not view the Incarnation in light of Redemption, but rather in light of divine glory.

It is only in the *Reportatio* version that Scotus expressly states that the Word would have become incarnate even if Adam had not sinned. In the *Ordinatio* version the discussion centers on the purpose for the Incarnation, and Scotus simply clarifies that the fall of Adam was not

---

[36] See Quodlibet 16 in *God and Creatures* pp. 380-387.

[37] Quodlibet 14, n. 16, 14.63 in *God and Creatures*, p. 332. See also *Ordinatio* IV, 49, q. 11, n. 9 (Vivès 21:417-18).

sine qua non for the Incarnation. Jesus Christ holds the center place in Scotus's understanding of the universe as freely created and redeemed by God. The treatment in Ordinatio III, 7, 3 illustrates the importance placed upon the humanity of Jesus as ordained (or preordained) for the glory of union with the Second Person of the Trinity. In his discussion, Scotus considers not what God would have done had the Fall not occurred, but rather what was the original intent of God relative to the Incarnation. On this he states that "the predestination of anyone to glory is prior by nature to the prevision of the sin or damnation of anyone."[38] God wills ordinately and thus first intends the end, then what is closer to the end. Thus, while Christ would not have come as "redeemer" had Adam not sinned, he would have come in the "highest glory" within creation. God intended first the glory as ultimate and final end, and then the Incarnation as leading to that end. In this, the creativity of the divine artist is seen. Since the order of execution reverses the order of intention, the union of human nature with the Word of God would take place in time prior to the achievement of final glory: the Incarnation would be in light of the glory, not in light of any sin which might be committed prior to it.

The Incarnation represents, then, not merely a divine response to a human need for salvation but rather God's intention from all eternity to raise human nature to the highest point of glory by uniting it with divine. This intention was an act freely chosen by God, and never necessitated by any human choice. Scotus affirms divine freedom for mutuality with humanity as an act of perfection, gracious magnificence and liberality. Mutuality between God and human persons is a freely chosen act initiated by God, foreseen from all eternity, begun in the Incarnation and fully realized at the Second Coming when Christ will bring all things together and God will be "all in all." The summit of creation is the communion of all persons with one another and with God. This is made possible by the union of divinity and humanity in Jesus Christ.

The centrality of Christ in the metaphysics of Scotus, both his position on the reason for the Incarnation and his defense of the Immaculate Conception, marks the capstone of his vision of human life and moral action. Christ is that very person in whom the human and divine achieve mutuality. He embodies the covenant between God and

---

[38] In Wolter, *Four Questions*, p. 30.

humans. He reveals how much God loves the created order. Our actions are pleasing to God, we are pleasing to God and loved with a preferential love. This is the basis for a second manifestation of divine freedom in human life: *acceptatio* and the order of merit. God freely accepts human actions informed by love and freely rewards them beyond strict justice. The goal of moral living is entrance into fuller relationship with God, into the deeper friendship called the order of merit. The necessity for grace in the completion of the human journey toward perfection is an important aspect which supports Scotus's insights. God is intimately present to the Scotist universe, both as epitome of creative freedom and as gracious judge whose acceptance (*acceptatio*) raises natural goodness to its supernatural reward.

The singularity of Scotus's vision of reality lies here. Against a philosophical perspective which emerged from the 13th century as typified by necessity of nature and universal, eternal and abstract truths,[39] Scotus elaborates an understanding of reality which celebrates freedom, contingency and attention to the particular. The basis for his emphasis on the superiority of theology over philosophy is precisely his preference for freedom over natural necessity as foundation for a cosmic order. Yet superiority does not mean independence, for the fruits of natural reflection are necessary in speculation on the data in revelation.

Scotus's discussion of human cognition supports his metaphysical insights on the value of contingent reality and points to the need for revelation in the human journey toward God. Because the human mind is limited and can only grasp being as being, divine self-revelation is necessary for any qualitative knowledge about God and as point of departure for any theological science. Despite this, divine revelation does not alter the natural human capacity for knowledge, nor will the beatific vision essentially change or replace the capacity of the human mind.[40] The

[39] Ludger Honnefelder, "Die Kritik des Johannes Duns Scotus am kosmologischen Nezessitarismus der Araber: Ansätze zu einem neuen Freiheitsbegriff", in J. Fried (Hrsg.), *Die abendländische Freiheit vom 10. zum 14. Jahrhundert*, Sigmaringen, 1991, 249-263.

[40] While we are capable of intuitive acts in the present state such intellection is imperfect. Present limitations will not obtain in eternity. "Still, I maintain that if we consider the nature of our intellect as a power or potency, its adequate or commensurate object is no more restricted than that of the angel. Whatever can be understood by one can be understood by the other." (Quodl. 14, n. 12, 14.43, p. 327). In its present state (*pro statu isto*) the created intellect is not capable of natural knowledge of God which is proper to the divine "haecceity".

vision of God fulfills the cognitive capacity of the human mind, it does not replace it with a totally different experience. Thus the scientific nature of theology is of the same rational status as that of philosophy, it is only the object which differs. In addition, intuitive and abstractive cognition belong to both philosophy and theology. They are activities of human cognition and do not differ in epistemic status, but only as to their principles, object and end.

Conclusion

It is not surprising, then, given this philosophical and theological background, that moral living for Scotus will be presented as imitation of divine selflessness and freedom, along with the joy of participation in a communal plenitude. The individual, so precious in the thought of Scotus, is never alone. Each person journeys back to God and joins with every other person along the way. For Scotus we are all *viatores* or pilgrims, making our way back home together. Moral living is life on the journey, involving mutual aid, for the journey is often difficult. Taking St. Francis's admonition to act always "as strangers and pilgrims"[41] Scotus holds that the journey is itself the goal: certainty of the arrival does not dispense with the need for right actions along the way. The success of the journey itself depends upon those actions which constitute each step.

Scotus sees the personal journey against a background of ordered reality and divine aid. Francis Kovach has argued that Scotus offers us a theory of *aesthetic* objectivity as a model for moral discussion.[42] This means that, for Scotus, all good acts are also beautiful, since goodness, like beauty, requires order, relationships and harmony among the dimensions of the parts within a whole. Scotus compares goodness to beauty, where proportion, arrangement and order are essential. We see this type of beauty around us in creation. All reality is ordered, Scotus affirms, by the hand of a loving and good Creator. God is the artist, cre-

---

[41] Later Rule of 1223, chapter 6. See *Francis and Clare*, Classics of Western Spirituality, Paulist Press 1982, p. 141.

[42] "In brief, Scotus seems to teach the real identity and the formal or logical distinction between the good and the beautiful. This, in turn, would mean the co-extensiveness of beauty with goodness and, since goodness is one of Scotus' simple transcendentals, the co-extensiveness of beauty with being." Francis Kovach, "Divine and Human Beauty in Duns Scotus' Philosophy and Theology" in *Deus et Homo ad Mentem I. Duns Scoti*, Rome 1972, p. 449.

ation is the work of art. Nothing exists out of relationship to everything else, "every being is ordered."[43] To be out of relation is absurd, it would mean existing all alone and in a vacuum.

Likewise, moral goodness consists of relationships of harmony and balance, and the morally good act is a beautiful whole of several dimensions, all joined together into forming the harmonious blending of human action which is most pleasing, especially to God. The moral person, then, is also an artist. She uses her skill in every situation to bring forth beauty in each act. This beauty requires a high level of reasoning as well as training, within the context of a moral community where values are shared and supported. In his emphasis on the moral as beautiful, Scotus offers a means for a rediscovery of the "lost transcendental," beauty, so important in classical thinking and so absent in moral discussion today.

In moral discussion, beauty is not simply in the eye of the beholder, according to Scotus. There is, he affirms, something objectively beautiful about a good action, something which anyone with reason can identify. The good action is pleasing to see, and fills the onlooker with real delight. This delight is both rational and affective. Thus, our affections do participate in moral judgment and moral living: they provide us with the joy we need to continue to act in reasonable and meaningful ways, in spite of difficulties we may encounter. The whole person, reason, intention, choice and affection, participates in the morally good act. The act and the person are both works of art created throughout a lifetime.

This is, of course, more easily said than done. Yet I highlight this aspect of Scotus's thinking to illustrate how optimistic he is regarding human nature, our place in the world, our capacity for goodness and the availability of divine help throughout our lives. For Scotus, this earth is a beautiful place to be, and we see its beauty around us at every moment in the order of the whole and the relationships among the parts. In addition, we are beautiful persons who long to express our internal beauty in external actions. We rejoice in goodness and are saddened by evil. Disharmony will occur, because although we long to be artists of quality, we often fail to accomplish what we intend. It is here that divine help makes up what is lacking in human effort. For Scotus, despair is never the hallmark of a moral person, for he knows that through it all, God

---

[43] "... for there is nothing in the universe which is not related by an essential order to the other beings, for the unity of the universe stems from the order of its parts." *On the First Principle*, 3.26, p. 56

continues to bring goodness out of every fragile human action. Hope and joy, then, are the two expressions of moral living.

While much of Scotus's discussion concentrates on the internal aspects of the human heart (especially motivation within human action), the dialogical model of Exodus 3:14 (God's self-revelation to Moses as being) creates the environment which calls for our response. The internal dimension exists in mutuality with the external, in the realm outside the individual moral agent. The external realm calls forth acts of responsible love and care. The moral domain is not an individual dimension of personal and private actions, it is a public forum where moral actions are the visible expression of internal reasoning and reflection.

Moral living for Scotus is dynamic. Just as God is a Trinity of persons in continual mutual relationship and love, so moral life is a constant attention to mutuality at all levels of human operation. Like the dancer or the athlete, the moral person is poised in readiness based upon heightened awareness of the value of every move. This readiness creates a positive tension which enables the dancer to perform and the athlete to execute the appropriate moves. Beneath the artistic tension is an internal place of balance and harmony, a place of peace, without which the artist could never perform.

This, then, is for Scotus the moral goal: to become artists of human living. It requires all that is best and most noble in the human spirit, it is not attained in a day but requires a lifetime. At the end, we shall resemble God, not in an abstract or inhuman perfection (which is sometimes seen as the moral ideal), but in the creativity of the artist in love with beauty and with reality around her. Simply put, moral perfection for Scotus is the perfection of loving. This other-centeredness is not destructive of self, but is rather that forgetfulness of self to which Jesus refers, when He states that it is the only way to enter eternal life.

two

Rational Freedom *and* The Will's Moral Affections

The key piece in any wind chime is the center disk. This must be adequately weighted to hang in a straight manner. It must also be light enough to be moved by the wind. The disk anchors the balance of the chime and makes possible the beautiful music. Like the disk, the will is the centerpiece of Scotus's moral discussion. It too is weighted with love for the good. It is balanced within itself by means of two innate moral affections: for goods of intrinsic value and goods of use. Scotus follows Anselm and calls them the affection for justice (*affectio justitiae*) and the affection for possession (*affectio commodi*). These moral affections manifest the complexity of rational desire which exists in a creative tension: when they exhibit internal balance there is self-control. This self-control informs all moral decisions with rationality.

There is also a deeper dimension to the will, one by means of which Scotus explains its capacity for self-movement. This is the order of freedom. In his discussion of freedom, Scotus relies on Aristotle's metaphysical account of rational causes. Together, the Anselmian discussion of moral affections and the Aristotelian analysis of rational freedom offer an explanation of moral action in which philosophy and theology cooperate. Anselm's perspective touches upon the reality of human experience. Aristotle provides a more scientific explanation of conditions in reality which make our experience possible. Both view the moral realm as one of rationality and freedom for self-control.

In 1951, Dom Odon Lottin published a famous study of the development of moral theology during the Middle Ages.[1] In this study, he identified two phases in the 13th century discussion of freedom and free will. Prior to 1250, thinkers focused upon the nature of free will (*liberum arbitrium*) and not upon the nature of freedom which is exercised in choice. Originally, Augustine's discussion in *De libero arbitrio* referred to free will as the faculty which is indifferent to good and evil, thus making sin the result of an act of free will. Anselm (✠ 1079) rejected this definition, noting that power to sin is itself an imperfection, and in his treatise *De libero arbitrio* defined free will as the power to conserve the rectitude of the will in view of that rectitude itself.[2] Free will is both rational and free to affirm what reason proposes. Right willing realizes the formal concept of liberty.[3] In other words, according to Anselm, I am most free when I act rightly.

The years between 1200 and 1250 produced a refinement of this question, as philosophers and theologians sought a better integration, raising questions about whether or not free will was distinct from reason and will or whether it joined the two as source or as product. Alexander of Hales (✠ 1245) considered it a power between reason and will which chooses but does not necessitate the consent of the will in execution. Odon Rigaud (1245) and Bonaventure (✠ 1274) both called it a free faculty: Bonaventure referred to the union of reason and will as *concors*[4] in free will. Aquinas (✠ 1274) saw it in light of the act of choice and called it a power identical to the will and impregnated with reason.[5]

The entrance of Aristotelian ethics affected the discussion around free will as well. Aristotle's texts were accompanied by Arab commentaries which, in general, painted the universe as operating out of cosmic necessity. Latin Masters in the Faculty of Arts after 1250 defended "astral determinism": the position that the stars affect, perhaps even determine, the decisions we make. Through the remainder of the 13th century, the moral question focused on the nature of freedom, especially after Odon Rigaud raised (and Bonaventure reprised) the question of the relationship of free will to deliberation about contingent

---

[1]   *Psychologie et morale aux XIIe et XIIIe siècles,* tome 1, Gembloux 1957, 11-389.
[2]   *Dialogus de libero arbitrio,* PL 158, 494B.
[3]   *Dialogus,* 501-2.
[4]   II Sent. 25, q. 5. See Lottin's discussion of this on p. 179.
[5]   Lottin, op. cit., 216.

acts. Odon stated, for example, that the blessed in heaven no longer possess free will since they no longer deliberate: they just love God freely. As early as 1267 the tradition following Bonaventure in the persons of Gauthier of Bruges and Gérard d'Abbéville (1269) affirmed the essential freedom and autonomy of the will.

The final years of the century witnessed a sustained defense of the will as immediate and autonomous cause of willing. The Condemnation of 1277 rejected astral determinism and reaffirmed the freedom of the will not to follow the judgment of reason, at least in this life. After 1277, the Franciscan voluntarist tradition emphasized reason as condition and will as unique efficient cause in the autonomous moral act. Evidence for this appears in the writings of Peter de Falco (1280-1282), William de la Mare, Richard of Middleton (1284) and Roger Marston. Henry of Ghent's *Quodlibet* 13 (Easter 1289) distinguished freedom from free will in the will: freedom relates to the end (as necessary) and free will is directed toward contingent means to that end. In other words, the notion of freedom deals more with the goal of human fulfillment, while free will has to do with concrete acts of choice over which I have some control. When I make choices, I exercise free will, not freedom.

In his discussion of the will's freedom, Scotus places himself within the tradition of medieval thinkers who defined rational freedom in light of the will's capacity for reasoning and choosing. Scotus remains faithful to the Franciscan position on the will as autonomous cause of the act of choice, and inserts the more recent reflection upon freedom within the earlier Anselmian context. His discussion unites reason and willing within the will and distinguishes it as a free cause from the intellect. In this, he presents his own understanding of *liberum arbitrium* as a single power within the will and as synonymous with the will.

Scotus's presentation of the will and the activity of willing freely involves two perspectives. The first is based upon experience: in the context of moral decision-making, we discover a creative tension between the two affections within the will. We are sometimes torn between the desire for right and proper action (Anselm's affection for justice) and the desire to protect or promote our own good (Anselm's affection for possession). The discussion reveals that these two affections constitute the will as a rational faculty. Scotus identifies the affection for justice as "liberty innate to the will," since it involves the internal self-control revealed by reflection upon internal experience. In this, his discussion of the will is largely indebted to Anselm and the pre-1250 legacy. The dis-

cussion is descriptive in nature and results from a sustained reflection
upon the activities involved in deliberative reasoning.

Scotus's second perspective examines the question of human freedom even further. The initial reflection on the two affections is followed by a deeper analysis of the nature of the will as a free cause. The
existence of the affection for justice is clarified by a philosophical consideration of different orders of causality: the necessary and the free.
Free causality, as an existing order, explains why the free will is a rational will, why the will is able to control itself, and why the will retains the
power to refrain from, to re-direct, to influence and to execute the
deliberative process at any point. The philosophical analysis of freedom does not replace, but rather enhances, the Anselmian discussion of
the two affections and the exercise of free will. In addition, Scotus links
the existence of free causality to the existence of a free first cause, without which no cause would be capable of self-movement. Ultimately,
Scotus's discussion of freedom leads to a discussion of divine freedom
and, as Paul Vignaux stresses, divine liberality and graciousness.[6] Were
there no first cause which operates freely, there would be no free
choice at all and, consequently, no moral dimension to human life. The
order of moral discussion hangs on the existence of an order of freedom.

The Divine Will

The exemplar for human freedom is, of course, the divine will.
God's free actions form the background and paradigm for Scotus's discussion of human freedom. God's freedom grounds human freedom,
provides moral objectivity and identifies the perfection of human freedom with imitation of and participation in divine activity. Correct
understanding of the will and freedom within Scotist thought is impossible in abstraction from consideration of divine perfection and acts of
choice.

In the case of creation, God's will provides both the metaphysical
and causal basis for the discussion of human freedom. The divine act of
creative freedom functions as exemplar for the perfection of rational
loving. God's choice to create this world was a free choice, not necessitat-

[6]   See his "Lire Duns Scot aujourd'hui" in *Regnum hominis et regnum Dei*, 1976, 33-46 as
well as "Valeur morale et valeur de salut" in *Homo et Mundus*, 1984, 53-67.

ed by any force other than the divine will itself. This world is not necessary, nor is it impossible that there might be other worlds. Consequently,
this world *as created by God* has value: the value of a realized project. This
world is the work of art which the divine architect has actually chosen to
create. Because there was a free choice at the beginning of creation, the
order of freedom permeates the created order. Side by side with the natural or necessary ordering of causes, there exists an order which operates freely and cannot be predicted.

The focus on God's freedom in Scotus's writings illustrates his personal reformulation of the notion and importance of willing, especially
after the Condemnation of 1277.[7] In his *De Primo Principio*, Scotus locates
the possibility of any free act in the necessity of a first cause which is
itself free. In Chapter IV, Scotus discusses the nature of God's actions *ad
extra* and the freedom which would be required for any free act to occur
on the level of human actions. Human free choice must be firmly
grounded upon divine freedom, for if the First Efficient (God) moves
necessarily, then no person would choose freely. The causal order would
only be a necessary one. Human actions would all be the result of determinism; we would have no power over our own lives, and no event
would be contingent. Everything would happen of necessity. If one
holds that the First Cause caused by an act of the will, then one must hold
that such an act was free. If not, there would be the logical contradiction
that the First Cause caused necessarily by willing. By definition, willing
must itself be a free act. Therefore, since there are other possible worlds,
and since this contingent world has in fact come into existence, then the
First Cause must have chosen to create freely. The existence of this freedom provides the possibility for the moral order.

> Therefore either nothing ever happens contingently, that is,
> unavoidably, or else contingency is there at the very outset in that
> even the immediate effects of the first cause are such that it was
> possible for them not to be caused.[8]

For Scotus, the nature of the divine will grounds the experience of free
choice in the human will. The question of the world's creation is not sim-

---

7   See my discussion of this in "The Condemnation of 1277: Another Light on Scotist
     Ethics", *Freiburger Zeitschrift für Philosophie und Theologie*, 1990, 37, 91-103.

8   4.18 in *A Treatise on God*, p. 84.

ply a matter for pedantic discussion: it has direct influence on the possibility of moral living.

But the divine will is not only the source for free causality, it is also
the exemplar for rational free choice. Scotus firmly unites divine willing to divine rationality and the perfection which this implies: justice
and liberality. Divine power is governed by the fundamental principle
of *praxis*. *Deus diligendus est* (God is to be loved). As a necessary axiom
for all moral judgment, even God chooses in accord with it. The present
order is good, not in and of itself, but because God has chosen to create
it. The created order has been chosen by God in light of divine infinite
goodness.

God's creative freedom did not cease once the world was in existence. God's freedom continues daily as it sustains all reality in being
and works to bring all reality into union with the divine persons. In the
moral realm, this happens in the divine act of *acceptatio*, or acceptance
and reward of human actions. By means of acceptance, God perfects
the order of human moral action by linking any act performed out of
love to an eternal reward. This reward is not measured according to
human standards of merit but far exceeds any concept of justice we
might entertain. "And so it is well said that God always rewards beyond
worth, universally beyond certain worth which an act merits... from gratuitous divine acceptance."[9]

For Scotus, divine freedom is not only creative freedom but also
redemptive freedom. The act of creation was only the beginning. It
extends through the Incarnation, redemption and acceptance to reach
fulfillment at the end of time when God will be "all in all." The dynamic
of God's relationship with our world is constituted by divine graciousness and not arbitrary actions. This is the divine exemplar for excellent
human behavior. God's actions are not simply free, but rational and
gracious.

An important aspect of divine perfection reveals itself in that creative freedom expressed in *firmitas* or constancy. God loves with an
everlasting love, which pours forth from divine goodness with a spon-
taneity and creativity and which gives all reality value. This eternal
commitment to love is both free (since creation does not have necessary
value in God's eyes) and a necessary implication of God's nature (since
God is infinite goodness). God's choice to love with a liberality beyond

[9]   *Ordinatio* I, 17, n. 149 (5:211).

human comprehension expresses what Scotus deems the most perfect manifestation of freedom: the constancy or commitment to remain steadfast.

William Frank has studied Quodlibet 16 as providing evidence of this notion of *firmitas* in Scotist thought. The nature of divine freedom is such that it remains even after a choice has been made: *firmitas* refers to the capacity to love a chosen object more deeply, with an intensity which deepens the commitment to that object.[10] It explains how the divine will can love the divine essence both necessarily (since the essence is absolute goodness and worthy of love) and freely (since the will is by nature a free potency, thus, all that it does is free).

> Furthermore, there are proofs of the reasoned fact to establish our claim. The first is this: action that has to do with the ultimate end is the most perfect. But freedom pertains to the perfection of such an action. Therefore, the necessity to be found there [in an act of divine love] does not do away with but rather demands what is needed for perfection, namely, freedom.[11]

Thus, as ordered toward the divine essence, the divine will necessarily loves the infinite good. However, as the perfection of loving, which must be directed toward the infinite good, the act is free, since it belongs to the will. The divine will loves freely the necessary object of its love, the divine essence. Only in God do the orders of necessity and freedom coexist in such an intimate manner. The divine will remains free, even when it loves necessarily. In such an act, the freedom of the will is intensified.

> Furthermore, an intrinsic condition for a power, considered absolutely or in relation to a perfect act, cannot be opposed to perfection in acting. Now liberty is an intrinsic condition of the will, either considered absolutely or as regards a perfect act. Therefore, liberty can coexist with that condition in acting that is the most perfect possible. Such is necessity, particularly where it is possible to have this. But it is always possible where neither of the extremes [the subject willing and the object willed] demands contingency in

---

[10] "Duns Scotus' Concept of Willing Freely: What Divine Freedom Beyond Choice Teaches Us" in *Franciscan Studies*, 42 (1982), 68-89.

[11] Quodlibet 16, n. 8, 16.32 in *God and Creatures*, p. 378.

the action between them [the willing]. Such is the case here [for the divine will].[12]

In other words, commitment in love does not remove liberty from the will, but rather intensifies it. Commitment may limit my options, but not my freedom. In fact, I have greater freedom within commitment than I do prior to choice. The divine will, in particular, continues to affirm its act of love as well as its acts of choice. This affirmation is a constant commitment which expresses the true nature of freedom.

On the human level, such constancy emerges from the correct balance between the natural/necessary and the free, thus between the natural and rational affections. Moral beings strive for such freedom and balance, not in an indefinite number of choices, but rather in the single choice of self-dedication and commitment, which must be renewed each day. Were we able to transcend time, we would only need to make the choice once, and it would determine our actions henceforth. However, we find ourselves within time where distractions lessen the intensity of our commitments. By renewing them each day, we choose to bring life to what might degenerate into stale, worn-out promises, which are kept long after they are meaningful, or, more often, simply forgotten.

The heart of Scotus's moral paradigm is that self-determination which is key to the notion of freedom. And yet, self-determination is not the moral goal, but only the first step to realizing what it means to be rational and to live a life of creative meaning and value. This goal is located in the free choice to commit oneself to another person, to a cause or vocation. It is only once this act is made that the human will truly begins to imitate God's highest perfection in love.

The Will's Constitution: The Two Affections

Scotus begins the qualitative discussion of moral choice with attention to human experience. His analysis here involves the theological, Anselmian discussion of the two affections within the will. This descriptive analysis of willing focuses on the data of everyday life: competing inclinations. The human desire to love can be caught among several goods: the different sorts of objects in the world (persons, money,

---

[12]   Quodlibet. 16, n. 8, 16.32, in *God and Creatures*, pp. 378-9.

power, popularity), concern for personal safety and self preservation, the higher desire to live a morally good life. These competing objects draw the attention of the will's affections in two ways. First, the affections for justice and for possession are directed toward objects within reality. These objects belong to an objective order of value, thanks to the power of the divine will. Second, the two affections deal with the development of character insofar as they relate to self-centered or other-centered concerns.

First, consider the external order. The object of the will is the good, and the discussion of the two affections arises from a reflection upon the nature of good objects and how they ought to be loved. Some objects have value as means to other, better ends. These objects are useful goods, called *bonum utile* in the Patristic and Stoic traditions. Money and food would be such goods. Their value belongs to their use, not to their intrinsic character. One could use or abuse money, using it to help the poor or hoarding it in the manner of Dickens's Scrooge. Goods of use can be lost without affecting the value or dignity of the one who possesses them. Status, power and prestige are all goods of use, since a famous person is no more a person than one who is ordinary.

There exist other objects which possess a type of absolute goodness or intrinsic dignity. These are called *bonum honestum*, or honest goods worthy of love not because of any use we make of them, but because of their internal value. These absolute goods ought to be loved in and for themselves, never possessed or used to further egotistical motives. Aristotle calls *eudaimonia* such a good; for Kant, the person possesses absolute value. Scotus identifies God as the primary candidate for this type of good and draws forth moral norms from the primary commandment to love God above all things and for God alone.

Next, let us look at the internal dimension. The affection for possession expresses the healthy concern for self sometimes called the self-preservation instinct. It can, certainly, become obsessed with self-related issues: health or power, for example. It can also be hampered by fears and anxiety. In itself, the affection for possession is not selfish: it can become selfish. The affection for justice focuses on others rather than self: it works to correct self-centered inclinations and broaden the rational journey to include right loving. As the external and internal dimensions interact, we might say that the affection for possession deals with objects whose value is judged as they relate to each individual: money becomes valuable to one who is avaricious, because it furthers the self-centered concerns of the person; food is valuable to everyone because it sustains life. Neither money nor food have intrinsic value determined in abstraction from use.

The affection for justice is the key moral desire within the will. It is the basis for calling the will *rational desire.* Allan Wolter identifies it as the basis for the Scotist contention that moral truth is accessible to natural reason.[13] As the will's higher tendency for justice or objective goodness, it represents the ultimate specific difference of the will[14] and thus its essence as free and rational. It makes the will a human will. The affection for justice expresses the rational desire to love others *as they deserve* and to the extent that they deserve, not from any profitability to be gained from them. The affection for justice is meant to govern the affection for possession, as a rational control over desire for the good:

> ...[the] affection for justice, which is the first checkrein on the affection for the beneficial, inasmuch as we need not actually seek that toward which the latter affection inclines us, nor must we seek it above all else (namely to the extent to which we are inclined by this affection for the advantageous)—this affection for what is just, I say, is the liberty innate to the will, since it represents the first checkrein on this affection for the advantageous.[15]

The interaction of these affections explains the type of freedom which the moral person experiences. While the affection for possession is a basic and good human instinct, we "need not actually seek" that to which we are inclined. The miser may be inclined to hoard money, but he does not have to act out of this inclination. The hot-tempered person may be inclined toward impatient outbursts, but does not automatically act out of this inclination. The freedom within the will is that of self-control, self-restraint. It is the first "checkrein" that rationality exercises on desire. This ability for self-restraint is innate within the will: it makes the will a rational will.

These two affections in the will are really dispositions toward loving. They are not "felt" affections, nor are they an emotional response to reality around us. They reveal themselves in emotional reactions, however. For example, the affection for possession is the source for the

---

[13]   Wolter, "Native Freedom..." in *Philosophical Theology,* p. 156.

[14]   Wolter, "Native Freedom...", p. 152.

[15]   *Ordinatio* II, 6, 2, n. 8 (Vivès 12:353-55). In Wolter, *Will and Morality,* pp. 469-71.

natural concern for self-preservation. When I feel threatened, my heart beats faster. This is the physical manifestation of my affection for possession in the instinct to protect myself. Scotus identifies the innate or natural freedom of the will (*libertas*) with the affection for justice. This is the rational desire I have for order in myself and in the world around me. The irritation I feel with chaos, the impatience I have with my own sinfulness, the determination with which I pursue a better social order: these all express my deeper affection for justice. It also manifests itself in my desire to stop before I act, think before I react.

Scotus departs from Anselm to affirm that the tendency toward loving justly (*affectio justitiae*) was neither lost nor damaged by original sin. The state of Adam and Eve before the Fall was not supernatural, but rather *preternatural*, somehow beyond our present condition but not on a par with God or the angels. After expulsion from Paradise, their condition was not sub-natural, but simply natural. Their wills continued to long for justice as they had prior to the Fall, only now there was less harmony between the two affections than before. As a reminder of their sin, Adam and Eve left paradise with an internal imbalance. Their human journey would require the re-harmonization between desires for self and desires for others. This reestablishment of harmony was not impossible, since the natural constitution of the will remained. It was, however, more difficult than before. Rational, ordered loving would now take longer to establish, and be harder to maintain.

Rational beings long for justice. This means appropriate loving and action. The rational affection calls an individual forth from self-interest to recognize others and to aspire to divine goodness. This affection for justice "tempers" the affection for possession: it nuances and governs it to consider the needs of others in addition to, and sometimes before those of the self. This tempering process is not automatic nor immediate. It takes place over time, and generally over a lifetime. It is a process which moves from self-determination to commitment.

When one is free *from* external compulsion, it is possible to act freely *for* value and commit *to* a life of integrity. Thus the self-determination Scotus locates in the will is only the beginning of a dynamic process of moral development. One is not free simply because one is not determined to do this or that, rather one is free to direct oneself toward values, in imitation of divine love and creativity.

The Nature of Willing and Free Causality

In addition to the Anselmian legacy, Scotus's discussion of the order of freedom enables him to take advantage of the wealth of philosophical and metaphysical analysis found in Aristotle. Because he uses Aristotle, Scotus can explain how freedom functions as a causal order within reality. For this, the Franciscan appeals to the discussion of causality found in the *Metaphysics*. Scotus uses this discussion to explain the nature of the will as a free cause superior to the intellect and capable of rational self-determination. This internal freedom reveals itself in the distinction between natural and free causality.[16] In his early *Subtle Questions on the Metaphysics*, Scotus discusses the difference between irrational and rational potencies. Their difference, he states, is identical to that between what is natural (or necessary) and what is free. Natural causes operate according to necessary laws and do not deviate from a pre-ordained effect; they have predictable results. Free causes, in contrast, are capable of self-determination and admit of different effects; their results cannot be predicted with any certainty.

> ...there is only a twofold generic way an operation proper to a potency can be elicited. For either the potency of itself is determined to act, so that so far as itself is concerned, it cannot fail to act when not impeded from without; or it is not of itself so determined, but can perform either this act or its opposite, or can either act or not act at all. A potency of the first sort is commonly called nature, whereas one of the second sort is called will. Hence the primary division of active potencies is into nature and will.[17]

The original text of Aristotle had presented rational and irrational potencies as distinct in terms of their effects. That is, rational potencies admit of more than one effect, while irrational potencies admit of only one effect. Humans make decisions which vary from time to time and situation to situation. Rocks, however, always fall in the same way.

---

[16] *Quaestiones in Metaphysicam*, IX, 15 (Vivès 7:606-617). An English translation of portions of this text appears in *Will and Morality*, pp. 144-172. In this text Scotus compares nature and will with irrational and rational potencies, respectively. Wolter's presentation and analysis of this text appears in "Duns Scotus on the Will as Rational Potency" in *Philosophical Theology*, pp. 163-180.

[17] *QQ Metaphysicam*, IX, 15, n. 4 (Vivès 7:609a). In *Will and Morality*, p. 151.

Scotus takes advantage of this original distinction and, defining the will as a non-natural (or free) potency, concludes that it must be rational.

> But if "rational" is understood to mean "with reason," then the will is properly rational, and it has to do with opposites, both as regards the acts it controls. And it has to do with opposites not in the way that a nature, like the intellect, acts, which has no power to determine itself in any other way. But the will acts freely, for it has the power of self-determination.[18]

Consequently, the will (a free cause) is superior to the intellect (a necessary cause), because the will is capable of self-determination and the intellect is not. And, since the will alone operates "along with reason," Scotus concludes that it is the only rational faculty. The intellect, in fact, is only rational when it operates with the will, that is, under the will's direction.

> And so if the intellect is called a rational potency, the aforesaid distinction [between rational and non rational] must be understood in the way explained above. For the distinction is not applicable to the intellect's own acts nor insofar as the intellect concurs with the acts of subordinate powers solely by means of its own act, for in both these ways it falls under the heading of "nature." Nevertheless it falls under the other heading insofar as earlier its own act is subject to acts of the will.[19]

In his discussion of Aristotle's distinction, Scotus emphasizes the singular nature of the will as free cause, and rejects those who claim that there is no such thing as a self-determining cause. These determinists look in vain for other examples of such free causality. Since they can find no other cause in nature which exhibits this quality of freedom, they deny that any type of free cause can exist. Scotus responds that this is precisely as it should be; there is no other example one can give because there is only one type of cause which is free. In order to discover it, we must engage in introspection and reflection upon our own acts of choice. When we do, we recognize that in performing any act, we "might have done otherwise."

---

[18] Ibid. n. 7, (7:611b), *Will and Morality*, p. 157.
[19] Ibid, n. 7, (7:611b) in *Will and Morality*, p. 157.

Such introspection reveals the internal control the will has over its own action. Scotus calls this the first act of the will: the freedom toward opposite acts. By this he means the freedom of the will to act or not, in Latin *velle* or *non velle*, to will or refrain from willing. A second freedom is directed toward "diverse objects," in Latin *velle* or *nolle*: e.g., choosing or rejecting an apple for a snack. A third freedom takes into consideration "diverse effects": e.g., long-term consequences of actions, such as good health through proper nutrition as opposed to eating whatever I feel like.[20]

A simple example reveals how complex the action of willing can be. When we look at a concrete action and reflect upon its several dimensions, we discover the levels of freedom to which Scotus refers. On a given afternoon, I may set out to complete one of several projects: work in the garden, work on this chapter, read a book. Prior to any decision about the use of my time, I must first move myself to act at all, and choose to choose from the above alternatives, rather than do nothing whatsoever. This deepest act of willing (the first act) is the choice to consider various ways of acting: to take them seriously as options. Here I choose to consider a matter for choice. Once I have decided to do something with my time this afternoon, then I consider my alternatives. At first glance, I may consider them according to my natural appetite: which one do I feel like doing, which one would require the most time or energy, which one might have the most return for my efforts. At this point in my personal deliberation, I see only the effect my action will have on me, for good or ill. My considerations might be called self-centered, without being narcissistic or selfish. A higher level of consideration would occur, however, if I turned my attention by an act of the will to consider the alternatives in terms of something other than myself: the possibility of enhancing the beauty of the garden, the good of others who might one day read this chapter, or the positive influence of the intellectual stimulus of reading a book, either for me or for others around me. These considerations move me beyond myself to consider the choice in a manner which is not determined by my relative fatigue level, or any tendency toward laziness, or any obsession with work, to reflect somewhat dispassionately upon the opportunities for action before me. As I work through my simple "deliberation process," I con-

[20] *Ordinatio* I, 38-9 (6:417).

sider more than myself and move outward in my reflections to consider consequences for myself and for others.

Scotus's discussion of willing takes into consideration all these levels of rationality within the will as a self-mover. He is, moreover, most concerned to demonstrate that the will, in its capacity for self-control, is a *sui generis* cause. Thus, it is unlike any other cause we can name. Throughout the reflection process described above, I could have interrupted my own deliberation at any time, or, once I had reached a decision, done nothing at all. The possibility for this can be explained by reflection upon the nature of willing, that is, through a sustained consideration of the nature of a cause which is itself unpredictable and unlike any other cause. Scotist thought affirms the value of the contingent and free, precisely insofar as free causality is itself superior to natural causality. There can be no case where necessary/natural action could be superior to free or contingent activity.

The dimension of self-control or self-determination, defining the realm of praise and blame, is the basis for the moral order. Insofar as the will is within its own control, it is capable of moral choices: choices for which it can be held responsible, at least to some degree. Freedom for self-mastery is then a significant element of moral goodness. Yet this is not the moral goal. The moral expert is not simply someone who acts in an autonomous manner. Self-direction does not constitute excellence. One could, for example, find a serial killer who might defend his life as one of self-directed action. Self-mastery is only the beginning. The life of moral training for value must accompany the choices, otherwise there would be no sense in which moral excellence would have the qualitative value of love. This training for goodness can only occur in mutuality with others who long for the same high quality of moral living.

The Functioning of the Will: Choice

The balance and mutuality of the two affections within the will is only one dimension of moral living. In addition, there is the process of willing, that activity of choice which seeks to move toward the perfection of freedom expressed in commitment. Here too Scotus identifies the interplay of two dimensions: the active and passive aspects of rational desire. Against those who, from a more intellectualist perspective like that of Aquinas, might consider the will to be only a passive appetite to be directed by the intellect, Scotus distinguishes within it both a passive (natural) and, more importantly, an active (free) aspect. "Properly speaking, however, the will is more than an appetite, because it is a free appetite coupled with reason...."[21] It is a desire which reasons. The natural or passive dimension can be understood more clearly when we compare it with other natural objects which tend toward perfection. One such example used by Scotus is the natural inclination of a stone to the earth's center, commonly identified with gravity. This is no different from the stone's weight. Hence, the will's natural inclination toward the good is no different from its operation as free, rational will.[22] The term *natural will* then, refers to the will insofar as it is inclined to its proper perfection (rational freedom),[23] just as a stone naturally inclines passively toward rest.

> The will can be considered doubly: as active, that is operative and choosing its act, or as passive, not insofar as it receives the act, but insofar as it is receptive of passivity for the supernatural, of which Augustine speaks in *De Moribus Ecclesiae*. Hence all passions of the will are reduced to love.[24]

This passive/active distinction enables Scotus to accept a definition of the will which places within it both the capacity for free choice (and thus mastery over its own acts) as well as an orientation toward God (and thus an openness to a perfection greater than itself).

The perfection of freedom in loving commitment, which begins in the will as self-mastery, is gradually realized via the will's natural love for the good in itself and with the help of grace. By virtue of its own acts of choice the will moves toward an increasingly better exercise of love for the highest good. This entire dynamic of moral *praxis* takes place against the background of divine goodness and within a context where the natural and supernatural collaborate. The harmony of grace with nature, a major concern for Scotus, is especially operative within the moral domain.

The concern to separate activity of the will from any sort of natural or necessary determinism by the intellect was a traditional stance taken

---

[21] III, 17, Codex A, in *Will and Morality*, pp. 180-1.
[22] III, 17, Codex A in *Will and Morality*, p. 180.
[23] III, 17, Codex A, *Will and Morality*, p. 182.
[24] Rep. IV, 49, q. 7, Codex A 280va. I am grateful to Allan Wolter for making this text available to me.

by most Franciscan thinkers of the 13th century. Scotus is not unique in the manner by which he so clearly distinguishes the will as a free potency, and identifies this ability for rational self-determination. What is significant is his concern to integrate reason and willing within the will by means of the Anselmian and Aristotelian perspectives. In both, he identifies freedom with rationality understood as self-control. The will is a rational, and therefore free, desire. Since the will is the only faculty which collaborates with reason, it alone, not the intellect, is the faculty proper to human persons. Rationality is the truest expression of freedom. Freedom is the summit of rationality.

Why Things Might go Wrong

The emphasis upon willing as the core to rationality was especially helpful to the Franciscans in dealing with the discussion of the reason for moral error (sin). The mainline Dominican tradition was much more intellectualist in its focus, explaining that moral error is basically the fault of the passions, which blind reason via the imagination. For the intellectualists, the will is only an appetite which becomes rational when directed (commanded) by the intellect. Freedom is located not in the will, but in the operation of reason which, when unencumbered by passion, could judge rightly. According to this understanding, the more dispassionate our reason, the higher the level of freedom and the better our moral judgments and choices. Moral education becomes primarily an intellectual affair which seeks to isolate reasoning from the passions.

Many Franciscans objected to this overly-intellectualist presentation of moral choices and sought to explain how, in the Garden of Eden, Adam and Eve could possibly have chosen to disobey God in light of the clarity of intellection they had. For men such as Bonaventure, Peter John Olivi and others, it was important to explain how saints are still free to sin, and how the most hardened sinner is never cut off from the possibility of conversion. In order to account for moral error, Bonaventure distinguished between acts of theoretical and practical judgment. He claimed that since the practical judgment does indeed direct the will to act, moral error is a faulty passage between the theoretical and practical dimensions. In other words, moral error involves an incorrect reasoning process between principles such as "Thou shalt not steal" and concrete judgments such as "this is an act of theft." The error results from a choice by the will, which somehow interferes with the intellect in its reasoning from theoretical to practical spheres.

Both Olivi and Scotus went a bit further, both to unify acts of judgment and to separate the will's choice from the result of rational reflection. Using the will's freedom to refrain from choice (*non velle*) as a basis, they affirmed that even in the presence of a judgment of reasoning, after a process of reflection and deliberation, the will is still free to choose counter to the verdict handed down. In addition, during the process of deliberation itself, the will can distract, stop and otherwise interfere with the processes of reasoning. In Book III, distinction 36 of the *Sentences*, Scotus states that correct judgment can exist in the intellect without correct choice in the will.[25]

> Hence one could give another answer, that this habit, generated by correct judgments, whether about the means to an end or about the ends themselves...is prudence, even though a correct choice does not follow. And then it would not be always necessary that a corresponding moral virtue be connected to a prudential judgment about some moral matter.[26]

It is important to understand the dual implication of such a position. On the one hand, this does indeed provide the necessary basis for sin. On the other hand, this position allows for an enhanced value to be conferred upon the freely chosen moral action. In other words, since the will is never forced to act in accordance with the conclusions of intellectual judgment, those times when it does agree to cooperate with what should be done become real manifestations of human excellence and goodness. For Scotus, in order to allow for the fact that a hardened sinner is able to convert he must defend a position which also provides for the saint to fall from grace by means of a free choice.

The Significance of Scotus's Notion of Freedom

Scotus's discussion of the nature of the will and the act of choice integrates reasoning and willing within the will by means of the two Anselmian affections and guarantees the potential for the will to

---

[25] Wolter presents this text in *Will and Morality*, pp. 405-411.

[26] *Will and Morality*, p. 411. The connection between prudence and the act of willing is discussed in chapters four and five.

choose counter to the judgment of right reasoning, thus providing the will with dominion over its own acts. His appeal to Anselm and the two affections clearly ties him to the Augustinian-Franciscan position on the superiority of the will over the intellect. His identification of *affectio justitiae* with rationality integrates reason within the will itself and provides a closer link between reasoning and willing, thus appealing to the discussion of free will prior to 1250. This discussion of free choice in the will relies upon an appeal to introspection and reflection upon the acts of deliberation and choice.

In addition, the discussion of the two modes of causality (natural/necessary and free) enables Scotus to offer a secure metaphysical basis for the will's self-determination in the concept of freedom. At the primary level within the will, freedom refers to the causality proper to willing. The will can determine its own activity, acting indifferently to external influence, because there exists at the source of causality an entirely free cause, God, whose creative act resulted in the contingent order. Divine freedom at the source of creation explains the existence of human freedom as the ability of the will to move and determine itself. While in God this freedom did in fact exist prior to the act of creation, in the human will it can only be discovered through reflection upon choice and upon the ability to refrain from choice.

Scotus's attempt to integrate pre-1250 free will discussion with post-1250 reflection upon freedom does not produce a theory which differs substantially from the Franciscan tradition in favor of the will. It does, however, focus the discussion on the divine will as the condition necessary for the existence of free causality. His defense of the rationality and justice in God supports the conviction that the divine choice for this world is eminently rational. The focus upon God also points to the importance of *firmitas*, or constancy, as a goal of the act of willing. The goal of free willing in the human experience is the sort of freedom which God always enjoys: ordered, rational and just. The seed of this is found in the nature of the will as a free cause but also in its constitution as an affection for justice and for the beneficial.

In presenting his understanding of the will, Scotus contextualizes the activity of choice. Seen as free will, the context is that of the two Anselmian affections. These both make up the will and are in a continual state of interaction within every occasion for choice. The two affections are for the good, either as good of use or good of value, as self-centered or other-centered. Deliberation is the interaction of the two affections in the will in the presence of the object. Proper or rational choice would be choice appropriate to the value of the object. Thus, free will for Scotus is never presented outside a context of deliberation and choice, and involves both rationality and control. In addition, to state that the essence of the will (as free) manifests itself in the two affections is not to affirm that each affection is somehow free and capable of eliciting acts of moral choice. This interpretation would produce two sub-wills within the will itself. It would result from the confusion of a descriptive mode of analysis with a causal explanation which functions as ground for the experience. There is no direct experience of freedom as a causal order within the will, only an experience of a power to choose otherwise: I might have acted differently.

Taken as freedom, the causality proper to the will appears within the context of divine free causality as source for creation and as exemplar for ordered and just loving. This causal freedom explains the ability of the will to choose counter to the judgment which emerges from deliberation and reflection. Thus freedom is identified at the level of execution as well as at the level of deliberation. This causal dimension of freedom allows for the possibility of sin, and explains how one might have both a correct judgment of reason and the appropriate control to do what is right, yet still choose counter to this judgment or refrain from action entirely. In addition, this freedom also explains why the will might choose counter to learned habits or judgments based upon vicious behavior. Scotus's discussion of freedom allows for the sinner's unpredictable conversion as well as for the saint's sudden fall from grace.

Freedom in Scotus does not refer to a quantitative discussion of options nor to a psychological state of inner awareness or harmony. Rather it defines a mode or order of causality which grounds the free will. Its source is in God the creator and its expression is in the structure of the act of willing as self-determined (*velle/nolle*), capable of self-restraint (*velle/non velle*) and rational insofar as it is self-controlled in the interaction of the two affections. While free will refers to the internal integrity of the will as a rational faculty capable of willing rightly, freedom refers to the causal order which grounds the will's ability to move from deliberation, through choice, to execution.

Scotus's understanding of the will is based upon his fundamental optimism about what it means to be human and about the basic human desire to love and be loved. His emphasis on the importance of freedom and the individual may give him a particular relevancy for today's moral discussion. The primacy of the individual and the rights of personal self-determination form the heart of the contemporary social and political context. Yet, as Bellah[27], MacIntyre[28] and Glendon[29] note, it is important to move beyond the radical individualism of today in order to discover the communal goods needed by all. Scotus affirms the existence and the primacy of freedom, but places this human and rational power within the larger context of mutuality and commitment. When rational self-control is developed, the ability for self-determination reveals freedom for values and for the integrity of commitment.

[27] Robert Bellah *et al, Habits of the Heart,* Berkeley: University of California Press 1985.

[28] Alasdaire MacIntyre, *After Virtue,* Notre Dame 1981, 1986.

[29] Mary Ann Glendon, *Rights Talk: The Impoverishment of Political Discourse,* New York: MacMillan 1991.

three

Mutuality and Harmony: Moral Goodness

While love is clearly at the heart of Scotus's philosophical enterprise, it is ordered and rational loving which constitutes the moral goal. Scotus clearly distinguishes between desire and love, stating that desire, while also an experience of the will, is not always ordered.[1] The rational act of love is an other-centered act, whose goal is not possession or use, but benevolence and charity. The noblest human act is love for the highest good. This act should not be motivated primarily by self-interest (*affectio commodi*) but performed out of respect for goodness as absolute and infinite (*affectio justitiae*). The goal of moral living is the perfection of such love, not only in regard to God, but to all persons as having God-given value and to creation as a divine gift.

The two-fold structure of affections within the will appears within the operation of human desire and love as it relates to the goods within the world according to use/possession or respect/honor. The rational person seeks to love goods of value in an appropriate manner, and to use certain lesser goods insofar as they promote goods of value. Such perfection of human loving both imitates the divine act of love (which loves all reality in accordance with its value) and emerges as the result of the process of self-perfecting loving within the will. This development

[1] "Furthermore, there is a twofold like or love, one which can be called love of friendship [benevolence], another called the love of desiring or wanting or coveting." II, 6, 2 in *Will and Morality*, p. 463.

47

of the natural human capacity for ordered love takes place under the direction of prudence, the primary virtue of the practical life.[2]

For Scotus, love for God is the self-evident first principle of *praxis.* Indeed, *Deus diligendus est* (God is to be loved) is that self-evident and necessary axiom according to which the entire cosmos (including divine activity) is ordered. While this principle is based upon the Aristotelian and Stoic maxim: "Good is to be pursued, evil avoided," it receives an obvious theological tone, once Scotus demonstrates that God is infinite being, and therefore infinite goodness.[3] To pursue the good is in fact to pursue God, the proper object of the human will.

This chapter continues the discussion of moral goodness in two key areas. First, the divine will appears as basis for moral order and rectitude. This larger, better framework of God's design replaces the impersonal Stoic eternal law. The rational will which pursues moral actions is itself measured by means of its relationship to divine rationality and freedom. This grounds the moral discussion in that of rectitude, or conformity to God's law. And yet, such a statement could betray Scotus's overall intent, for it is not the divine law which dominates moral discussion, but the divine lawgiver, as the personification of rational judgment and the eternal exemplar for human moral life. The emphasis on divine activity, rather than divine action, creates a dynamic moral perspective, and the moral expert (like God) is described as an artist whose activity generates excellence and character. Second, in Scotus's presentation of the morally good act as a work of art, we find the particularly aesthetic dimension of the Franciscan's ethical thinking. The artistic emphasis unites the human moral agent to the divine exemplar: in acting morally we image divine creativity. In this chapter we also continue the imagery of the wind chime, for this aesthetic dimension appears in the discussion of moral goodness both as visual beauty and musical harmony.

---

[2]   "... the intellect is perfected most perfectly by prudence, if that virtue is most perfect. For then one would have the most perfect practical knowledge about every possible action and under every possible circumstance." III, suppl. D. 34, in *Will and Morality,* p. 355.

[3]   This is his project in the *Treatise on the First Principle.*

Natural Knowledge and the Moral Law

For Scotus, moral goodness is presented as the beautiful whole comprised of an action and the circumstances which surround it. Moral rectitude refers to the relationship of the act as a judgment of right reasoning in relationship to the moral law. Objective moral goodness is not measured by the human rational will, but rather by the divine will as expressed in the principles contained in the commands of the Decalogue.

For the medievals, human reason has access to knowledge of moral principles through both natural and revealed orders. Creation is a great book written by God in which human reason can read the order of the cosmos and conclude something about God's goodness. In addition, the Bible is a second, smaller book in which key information can be found, information not found in nature. This deals with God as Trinity and with Jesus as Incarnate divinity. God has provided us with these two ways of discovering the hidden truths of reality. Creation is the most immediate and reveals God the Artisan. Peter Lombard had formulated this insight as follows:

> That the truth [about the *invisibilia Dei*] might be made clear to him, man was given two things to help him, a nature that is rational and works fashioned by God. Hence the Apostle says [in Romans 1:19] "God has revealed to them," namely, when he made works in which the mind of the artisan somehow is disclosed.[4]

Allan Wolter identifies the influence of Hugh of St. Victor on the Franciscans, especially relating to the application of this insight to the ethical sphere and to the divine will. Hugh had written:

> Was it not like giving a precept to infuse into the heart of man discrimination and an understanding of what he should do? What is such knowledge but a kind of command given to the heart of man? And what is the knowledge of what should be avoided but a type of prohibition? And what is the knowledge of what lies between the two but a kind of concession, so that it is left up to man's own will where either choice would not harm him? For God to command, then, was to teach man what things were necessary for him, to pro-

---

4   *Sentences* I, Dist. 3, c. 1, p. 69, quoted in *Will and Morality*, p. 25.

hibit was to show what was harmful, to concede was to indicate
what was indifferent.[5]

The fundamental principles of moral living, embodied in the
Decalogue, are written on the human heart and reducible to the maxim
"Do good and avoid evil."

Deus diligendus est (God is to be loved) expresses the first principle
of the moral domain. It belongs to natural law and admits of no excep-
tion. An action which is motivated by love for God and by the desire to
promote God's glory is morally good, even where it cannot be
executed.[6] The moral question for Scotus focuses on the question of
motivation. Why we do what we do, and whether or not our action is
informed by love for God, are more important than what we do. Scotus
provides a simple example in the act of almsgiving. This action may
admit of several motivations.[7] One might have the mere desire to
appear generous in the eyes of others; one might perform the act out of
fear. The highest moral motivation, however, derives from the nature
of the act itself: generosity to the poor out of love is itself an appropriate
moral act, because God has commanded that we love one another. It
belongs to the highest and purest moral motivation to perform such an
act simply because it is the right thing to do.

As first principle, the command to love God above all belongs to
the generalized body of knowledge called moral science. This knowledge is accessible to the human will via the *affectio justitiae.* As we saw in
the last chapter, such moral truths are grasped by the will insofar as it is
rational, that is insofar as it operates "with reason," having any control
over its own acts. The will is constituted to seek the good as known in a
manner which is not necessitated by any external force, but which is
realized according to self-determination. In other words, persons who
wish to pursue a moral life pose questions to themselves about the value

[5] PL 176:268. Quoted in *Will and Morality,* p. 25. Wolter continues: "That Scotus
    accepted this principle is clear from what he says about the law of nature being, in
    the words of St. Paul, "written interiorly in the heart" (*Ord.* I, Prol., n. 108; Vatican
    1:70; also II, dist. 28)." ibid.

[6] "Indeed, the decision to do something for a worthy purpose is no less good when
    the external act that ensues fails to achieve that end than when it succeeds."
    (Quodlibet 18, n. 6, *God and Creatures* 18.15, p. 403).

[7] See the discussion of this in II, 7, nn. 28-30. Wolter provides an English translation
    of a section of this question (nn. 28-39), *Will and Morality,* pp. 218-225.

of the goods which surround them. They seek to love justly, in accord with an objective order. They want to love the highest good in the most perfect manner: they want to love God with their whole heart and mind. They also want to measure their own actions according to God's will for them. For Scotus, this is what rationality means: this is the fulfillment of the moral journey.

The central moral issue for Scotus, then, is found not in identifying objects which are good (since all creation is both good and ordered), but rather working out the adequation of loving relative to each object, and thus increasing the harmony of *affectio justitiae* with *affectio commodi.* The most perfect moral act is sincere love for God, because God is infinite goodness and, as such, the object most worthy of such love.

> As for the first, I say that to love God above all is an act conformed to natural right reason, which dictates that what is best must be loved most; and hence such an act is right of itself; indeed as first practical principle of action, this is something known per se, and hence its rectitude is self-evident. For something must be loved most of all, and it is none other than the highest good, even as this good is recognized by the intellect as that to which we must adhere the most.[8]

This desire to love God does not just belong to a narrow class of believers. In fact, all persons desire to love the highest good in an absolute manner. If we acknowledge any order in the world around us, any scale of values, we implicitly acknowledge the existence of a first: a highest value. Because we are rational, we want to love this highest good most perfectly.[9]

Scotus not only identifies this highest good with a personal God, but, unlike other scholastic thinkers who followed Augustine's Stoic account of eternal law (*lex aeterna*), goes a step further. He personifies the moral law by linking it overtly to the divine will. He replaces the Stoic emphasis on an eternal law of nature with a discussion of an eternal lawgiver whose will constitutes the present order (*de potentia ordinata*) but who could have acted otherwise and created a different moral universe (*de potentia absoluta*). Law is a function of a legislator, not of an impersonal

---

[8]   *Ordinatio* III, suppl. dist. 27, established by Wolter on the basis of Codices A (ff. 171ra-72rb) and S (ff210va-12rb), in *Will and Morality,* p. 425.

[9]   *Will and Morality,* p. 435.

necessity.[10] This means that, for Scotus, the Ten Commandments should never be read as impersonal obligations, but as the expressed, personal desire of the eternal Lawgiver. To obey the law is to commit oneself to a relationship with a divine community of Persons. The central law is the command to love.

Love for God constitutes the first commandment, love for neighbor the second. The two great commandments are not of the same status, however, since the second does not follow directly from evident practical principles, but is rather the command of the divine Legislator. Here again we see Scotus's insistent commitment to divine freedom. The command to love our neighbor is in harmony or *consona* with the command to love God. God desires that we love others as expression of our relationship with the Persons of the Trinity. We observe the first commandment by and through our love for others, not because it is a necessary consequent of the first, but because God has revealed it to us. "... [T]his precept "love your neighbor as yourself" is understood not as it is derived from the first practical principle of the law of nature, but as the Legislator meant that it be observed...."[11]

The Relationship of the Divine Will to the Law

Such a focus on the divine intent in the law enables Scotus to distinguish between the commands of the first table of the Decalogue and those of the second. While the first three commandments deal with God, the last seven do not, at least not directly. These deal with the neighbor and are grounded, states Scotus, not directly in the absolute value of the person but in the absolute goodness of the divine command. The first command, "God is to be loved" is an analytic truth of natural law, since God is infinite goodness and thus alone worthy of absolute love. The second and third commands are derived from this first and in this way belong to natural law strictly speaking (*stricte loquendo*).

The last seven commands relate to the neighbor and, thus, do not hold the strict status of absolute moral principle.[12] They do, however,

---

[10]   See Wolter's discussion of this in *Will and Morality*, pp. 21-5.

[11]   III, 37, unica, n. 12 (Vivès 15:845a).

[12]   His discussion of private property makes his position clear. If there were in positive law the following principle, "peace is to be maintained among members of a community", one could not conclude necessarily that "each member should enjoy

represent the intention of the divine lawgiver, specifically as to the practical implications of obedience to the first command. According to the present contingent order, the command to love God is best followed through acts of love for the neighbor. These acts include respect for parents, life, property, reputation, truth and the dignity of marriage. Although these commands are not absolute, they are in harmony (*valde consonant*) with the first command. Scotus does not view the last seven commands as absolute, because nothing other than God is worthy of absolute love. By separating the two tables of the law, he is better able to deal with the actions of God recorded in the Bible, particularly related to the thorny question of divine dispensations.

Scripture records a limited number of specific cases where God commanded acts which were against the Decalogue. For example, in Genesis God commands Abram to sacrifice Isaac and to take Hagar as his second wife, and in Exodus God commands the Hebrews to despoil the Egyptians. These commands are in direct contradiction to the fifth commandment ("Thou shalt not kill"), the sixth commandment ("Thou shalt not commit adultery") and the seventh commandment ("Thou shalt not steal"). The issue here is significant, for its solution depends directly upon the understanding one has of the nature of law and moral principle.[13] Scotus sees both as personal, not impersonal, realities which depend upon the will and specifically, the divine will. Thus, in the above mentioned cases, God declared licit what had been formerly (or generally) seen as illicit.

Scotus's solution to this question of divine commands to perform illicit acts centers on his distinction between the two tables of the Decalogue. Strictly speaking, there can be no moral command for any person to hate God. However, speaking more broadly, the other commands could be dispensed with, and the subsequent action deemed moral, if the divine Lawgiver saw fit. Of course, only God could declare such a dispensation, since the divine will constitutes the natural order.

---

private property". There is no necessary connection between peace and private property, however, Scotus admits that laws protecting private property do in fact promote peace among citizens. Private property is not an absolute right, and certain circumstances may occur which require the relinquishing of personal property. See III, 37, unica, n. 8 (Vivès 15:827b).

13 On this, see Robert Prentice, "The Contingent Element Governing the Natural Law on the Last Seven Precepts of the Decalogue, According to Duns Scotus" in *Antonianum*, 42 (1967), pp. 259-292.

Scotus's solution places increased value upon divine freedom and the personal, relational dimension to natural law. In the act of divine dispensation, God sets the law aside and declares a normally illicit act licit for this person and in these circumstances.

We might appreciate Scotus's discussion here by comparing it briefly to the parallel treatment found in texts of Thomas Aquinas.[14] For Aquinas, the dispensations recorded in Scripture are not real but only *apparent* transgressions from the law. The Dominican emphasizes the intention of the law rather than the letter of the law, and observes that in some cases the letter of the law must be broken for the intention or spirit of the law to be fulfilled. Consequently, Aquinas sees no need to separate the natural law into two categories, and refers to all ten commandments as part of the natural law *stricte loquendo*, thus admitting of no exceptions.

While Aquinas affirms the intention of the law, Scotus underscores the mind of the lawgiver. The difference here may be slight, but the implications are significant, since they point to the difference between a depersonalized cosmos governed by necessity, and a personal universe based upon freedom and love. Scotus offers a more personal basis for the Stoic legacy of *lex aeterna* and thus personalizes obedience to moral principles. When I follow or obey the law embodied in the Decalogue, I am not merely moved by abstract moral principle or values, but rather by the conscious desire to remain in relationship with God. Moral living is at heart relational living which joins person to person and person to God.

A second implication deals with the "ecumenical" aspect of Scotus's moral theory. As Allan Wolter points out, in the distinction between natural law *stricte loquendo* (commands 1-3) and *large loquendo* (commands 4-10) Scotus remains coherent in his thinking without requiring narrow legalism.

> Thus, although Scotus's ethical system does presuppose knowledge of the existence of God, it is in a sense independent of any particular special revelation on the part of God....Also, the Judaic or Moslem believer, or any other ethician who grounds moral obligation on the will of God as revealed to him by a rational analysis of human nature, might still agree with Scotus's funda-

---

[14] *Summa Theologica* Ia-IIae, 100, 8.

mental conclusions about what is morally right in our dealings with our fellowmen without necessarily accepting the whole of what he believed God has revealed to him through the Scriptures and positive divine law.[15]

Hence, while Scotus's discussion of the relationship of the law to the divine will places him squarely within a Divine Command Tradition, he remains a thinker whose ideas are strong enough to be attractive to traditions other than Christian. His moral presentation of law neither requires adherence to Christianity nor to any specific aspect of Christian revelation. I would add that a discussion with Scotist moral thinking requires some commitment to a personal, loving God and a communitarian approach to moral questions.

The Morally Good Act as a Work of Art

Scotus insists upon the primacy of God's will for an objective moral order. He affirms the centrality of the human will in self-determination. Moral goodness reveals itself between these two wills as a work of artistic creativity. This creativity requires some standard for excellence: this is the divine will. The human will certainly does not define goodness every time it chooses. While this does characterize the divine will, the finite will has no such moral authority. Although the presence of *affectio justitiae* within the natural constitution of the will establishes the possibility for a self-perfecting moral dynamic, there is much more to the Scotist presentation than the interaction of two human affections. The discussion of moral goodness focuses on the relationship of goodness to beauty. It presents the moral act as a work of art and the moral agent as an artisan.

One need not look far within philosophical texts to discover the importance of an artistic model for moral discussion. Aristotle's *Nicomachean Ethics* presents art as well as medicine as an appropriate image for moral living. Book I presents practical excellence as "an activity in conformity with virtue" via the analogy of a musician: "...the proper function of a harpist, for example, is the same as the function of a harpist who has set high standards for himself" (1098a9-10). This same image returns in Book II where Aristotle begins his discussion of virtue with an investigation of the relationship between the attainment of

---

[15]   *Will and Morality,* pp. 28-9.

excellence and habitual action:

> For the things which we have to learn before we can do them we
> learn by doing: men become builders by building houses, and
> harpists by playing the harp. Similarily, we become just by the
> practice of just actions, self-controlled by exercising self-control,
> and courageous by performing acts of courage. (1103a34)

Although the musical and artistic imagery appear early in the *Ethics*, the
references to medicine are by far the more numerous. Medical images
are used heavily in Book I to describe the end of ethics, particularly in
the elucidation of the concept of *eudaimonia* (human excellence or fulfillment).[16] The method proper to such a practical science as ethics
resembles that of medicine insofar as too much precision would exceed
what the subject matter permits (1104a4 and 1141b15-20). Finally, the
moral expert resembles the physician who makes judgments relative to
the goal of health for the soul (1138b30-33 and 1105b18).

Both Aquinas and Scotus use Aristotelian imagery in their discussions of moral excellence. Thomas, with his emphasis on the natural
desire and its necessary relationship to beatitude as moral goal, tends to
favor the image of health as central to his discussion of moral goodness.
In his *Sententia Libri Ethicorum*, Book I, lectio 9, Aquinas highlights the
importance of the ultimate end as well-being and emphasizes its simi-
larity to physical health. "On this we should first consider that there
seem to be different goods aimed at in the different activities and skills.
The good aimed at in medicine is health, the good aimed at in the military arts is victory, and in every other art some other good."[17] The relationship of lesser to more ultimate ends is described with the example
of bitter or pleasant-tasting medicines (useful goods) to health (a more
complete good). While Aquinas does not ignore the musical imagery
(he refers to both flutist and harpist in lectio 10), its examples are less
frequent.[18]

---

[16] At 1094a7, 1094b24 and 1097a16-18.

[17] *Sententia Libri Ethicorum* I, lectio 9 in *Opera Omnia*, vol. 47:31. The English is taken
from *The Philosophy of Thomas Aquinas*, edited by Christopher Martin. London:
Routledge 1989, p. 170.

[18] A glance at the *Index Thomisticus* reveals a ratio of health to art images at about
three to one. It is true that Aristotle himself favors the medical imagery, so
Thomas's terminology is not that surprising.

Scotus makes greater use of the artistic image of the musician and harmonizes the notion of creative freedom with moral goodness. This preference for art rather than medicine as model for his discussion of moral excellence reflects his preference for freedom over natural necessity. In addition, he rejects any natural or necessary connection between knowledge of an objective moral goal such as *eudaimonia* and the human ability to attain it in this life (*pro statu isto*). He is skeptical about the possibility of a successful philosophical model for moral living based upon happiness. True happiness can only occur in light of an eternal reward, when the human heart finds at last the infinite goodness and beauty of God for whom it longs. But this dimension does not lie within the domain of philosophical speculation: believers know its truth because of revelation.

Scotus removes any reference to necessary fulfillment in an eternal reward from moral discussion and focuses his attention on the concrete act seen in all its particularity as morally beautiful. The morally good act appears not as a means to a pre-determined end, but as an artistic whole within which harmony and proportion among several elements exist. The morally mature person imitates divine creativity in producing beautiful acts and a beautiful character. This discussion does not deny the ultimate fulfillment in eternity, it simply postpones discussion of supernatural reward.

Scotus defines moral goodness as a decoration in *Ordinatio* I, 17; he affirms that the morally good act is a beautiful whole comprised of several elements within an appropriate relationship to one another and under the direction of right reasoning.

> ...one could say that just as beauty is not some absolute quality in a beautiful body, but a combination of all that is in harmony with such a body (such as size, figure, and color), and a combination of all aspects (that pertain to all that is agreeable to such a body and are in harmony with one another), so the moral goodness of an act is a kind of decoration it has, including a combination of due proportion to all to which it should be proportioned (such as potency, object, end, time, place and manner), and this especially as right reason dictates.[19]

This visual imagery locates beauty and moral goodness in the propor-

---

[19]   *Ordinatio* I, 17, n. 62 (5:163-164). In *Will and Morality,* p. 207.

tion of parts within a greater whole. It is the proper ordering of elements within a given visual field. This means that, like a beautiful land-
scape, all parts of the moral act "fit together," they form a unit which is
beautiful to look at. These elements or parts can be identified as timing,
method, motivation, etc. Every particular moral act has the same
requirements of balance and harmony among the aspects which constitute it. Like the wind chime, the moral act is a balance of individual
pieces within a larger configuration of beauty.

Scotus goes even further in the *Reportatio* version of this same question. In this later text, he brings in divine appreciation of this beauty.
God accepts each soul because it is beautiful.[20] But this was not a later
Scotist insight. In the earliest *Lectura* version, he calls the virtue of charity a spiritual decoration which embellishes the soul whose act is pleasing to and therefore accepted by God.[21]

The entire Scotist discussion of goodness involves intricate levels of
relationships and reveals a dynamic vision of beauty with mutuality at
its core. Throughout, the Franciscan integrates as many elements as
possible into his discussion, as he examines how they interact to promote harmony in human living. The *Ordinatio* I, 17 definition of moral
goodness as "the harmony of all circumstances [belonging to an act] in
accord with right reason" blends mutuality, virtue, consequences and
principle within an aesthetic model.

When Scotus refers to "all the circumstances" which belong to an
act, he appeals to Aristotle's discussion in the *Nicomachean Ethics* where a
good act is seen in terms of several converging factors: goal, object, time,
place, manner and consequences. The morally perfect act is done for
the right reason, at the right time and place, according to the right manner and taking all significant consequences into account. The circum-

[20] *Rep. Par.* I, 17, q. 2, n. 9 (Vivès 22:211b).
[21] *Lectura* I, 17, n. 59 (17:201). Francis Kovach explains the relationship of virtue to the
     soul: "Considered relatively, moral beauty has the character of ornament, because
     it is something extrinsic and added to the human act in such a way as to beautify
     that act and, through the act, the human soul itself. The human act is, however, not
     the sole proximate subject of moral beauty to Scotus. For he speaks of the moral
     beauty both of the human act and of the moral virtue. It is this virtue from which
     the soul receives its moral beauty with relative permanence; and in turn, it is this
     relatively permanent moral beauty for which God mainly loves the soul." "Divine
     and Human Beauty in Duns Scotus's Philosophy and Theology" in *Scholastic
     Challenges to Some Mediaeval and Modern Ideas*, 1987, pp. 102-3.

stances surrounding a given moral act may vary from one situation to another: the appropriate course of action must be determined by the operation of right reasoning. For example, while lying is wrong, telling the truth is not always appropriate. Sometimes even telling "the whole truth" would do more harm than good. The rational person is capable of determining when the truth should be told, and to what degree the truth should be told. In a similar manner, it is possible for an act to be morally appropriate in private and not in public.[22]

For Scotus, there are only two types of actions which are unconditionally wrong: hatred of God and perjury.[23] While he presents these as two different types of acts, it is not hard to see that the second is closely related to the first. The first is wrong because God is infinite goodness: goodness must always be loved. The second is wrong because when I commit perjury, I call upon God to bear witness to the truth of what I say. At the same moment, my intent is to deceive. Thus, I ask God to join me in a lie. This is, of course, an insult to God's nature as Truth. It is using God for my own ends and, thus, can never be done out of love for God.

The most fundamental dimension of goodness in a moral act relates to its objective quality. By objective, Scotus directs attention to the object of the action. For example, in the directive "tell the truth," truth is the object of the action. "Love your neighbor as yourself" is an objectively good act because persons (both you and your neighbor) are worthy of love. "Protect life" is a moral command, because living beings have value. Every moral action has a "natural objective dimension" which can be identified if we reflect on what is being done and to whom.

But this objective dimension does not exhaust the moral beauty of the action. In addition, there is the free quality of an act chosen by someone. In other words, I might tell the truth or love my neighbor simply because someone in authority has told me to do so. These acts would be "objectively good" but they would not be the result of my own free choice; they would not enhance my moral character. In fact, I might not even pay attention to what I am doing. However, when I undertake to live the moral life for myself, then my actions take on a free and rational quality which enhances their natural objective goodness. Then, in telling the truth, I am not simply performing a good action; I am becoming a better person.

[22] III, 38 in *Will and Morality,* pp. 481-501.
[23] III, 39 in *Will and Morality,* pp. 501-519.

The object is a primary and fundamental dimension to the morality of any action. It is the place where the moral discussion begins. Moral
objects are human goods which can be identified by reflection on what
it means to be human. Scotus clarifies this reflection process in
Quodlibetal Question 18, where he moves from a discussion of those
objects proper to a rational agent (truth, for example) to the affirmation that some objects and activities, by their nature, are proper human
goods. The proper human goods fulfill us. Scotus gives the example of
the human intellect, human nature and the act of understanding.
"Knowing what it means to attain knowledge, it would also be clear to [a
person] what it is not appropriate for his mind to reach."[24] No one enjoys
being deceived, least of all the inveterate liar. Because we are rational,
we seek reasonable explanations for human behavior, explanations
which exhibit consistency, coherency and rationality. In addition,
everyone desires goodness, even though sometimes we can be mistaken
about all the consequences of certain actions seen to be good. The chain
smoker, for instance, does not long for death, but rather for the pleasure found in smoking. The addict finds some pleasure in the addictive
behavior, and does not choose it because of the health risks or the with-
drawal pains experienced when the behavior is altered or ended. Thus,
the truth and the good (either real or apparent) are significant moral
objects; they are human goods. Indeed, truth and goodness are the two
most fundamental moral objects; they respond to our human aspira-
tions which express themselves in activities of knowing and loving.

Because of the importance of the object in the initial determination
of moral goodness, Scotus suggests that some acts may be "indifferent"
or morally neutral. These are acts whose object is not inappropriate or
irrational, but which all the same is not appropriate in a moral sense. By
"indifferent" Scotus refers to an act performed in the absence of moral
intent. This happens "where the act is referred to the end only habitually or not at all."[25] Thus, there are some human acts which, though freely
chosen, do not fall into the category of "moral" for lack of an appropriate object of desire. Scratching one's chin, for example, while freely
chosen, is not to be considered under the aspect of morally good, since
the object of the action (relief of the itch) is morally insignificant. "This
is proved first from the Philosopher in II *Ethics*. The habit of justice is

---

[24] *God and Creatures* 18.13, pp. 402-3.

[25] In *Will and Morality*, pp. 231-3. "...such as stroking the beard or brushing off a bit of
straw and suchlike." p. 233.

not produced by doing what the just do, but by doing such things in the way that the just do them." (II, 41)[26] Conscious intent to perform a moral action in a moral manner is key to the moral act. It is not just doing what good people do, it is acting as good people act and for the same reason that good people act. In the truly moral action, character is joined to performance, motivation to action.

In itself, the morally good act resembles not simply a whole, but a beautiful whole thanks to the developed ability of the moral expert in identifying significant data in light of principles, objects and circumstances. In addition, the moral expert acts out of the appropriate moral motivation. The deliberation proper to moral judgment can be compared to the activity necessary to produce a work of art which has visual balance and proportion. The expert has a developed eye for beauty and seeks to create beauty in each act and moral judgment.

Moral Goodness as Musical Harmony

Scotus does not simply provide visual imagery in his discussion of moral goodness. To the visual dimension he adds the auditory: moral goodness is like harmony in music. Like music, the morally good act is itself the result of a dynamic harmonization of several elements which vary from one act to another. This intricate and dynamic harmony of goodness extends beyond the moral act considered in itself. Properly understood, the moral dimension is only one aspect of multiple goodnesses which can be identified in human action. In Quodlibetal Question 17, Scotus places the rational or moral dimension of a good act within a larger dynamic of goodness. He identifies four possible aspects of goodness: the natural, moral, charitable and meritorious.

> In this connection note the order that obtains between the bare act to which blame or praise is imputable, the virtuous act, which stems from moral virtue, the charitable act, and the meritorious act. The first expresses a relationship to the potency which freely elicits the act; the second adds to this a relationship to the virtue which inclines to such an act, or rather to the rule of virtue, i.e., a dictate of right reason; the third expresses a relationship to charity which inclines the will to such an act; the fourth adds a relationship to the divine will which accepts the act in a special way. The third adds

[26] Quodl. 18, n. 7 in *God and Creatures*, p. 405.

some goodness over and above that conferred by the second and is itself required for the fourth, not indeed by the very nature of things, but rather by a disposition of the accepting will.[27]

To the natural and moral goodnesses we can add the charitable motivation and divine acceptance. Charitable motivation means that the act is not only rational but performed out of love. Here, I tell the truth not just because the truth should be told, not simply in the way a good person would tell the truth, but because I love the truth, because I love the person to whom I am telling the truth. This is distinct from "telling the truth on principle." This loving action is personalized and creates a relationship between me and the other.

Divine acceptance means that God sees and is pleased with my act of telling the truth in love. God's pleasure is creative of relationship as well: the relationship of reward. When I perform any good action out of love, God responds to reward me. In this life, I am not aware of the exact nature of this reward. It lies hidden with God and will only be revealed to me when I see God face to face.

These last two dimensions of the action both belong to the order of love: my love for others and God's love for me. This love does not replace the other orders of goodness. In fact, loving motivation depends upon the natural goodness of the act, upon its objective appropriateness. I cannot perform any act I please "out of love," I can only perform good acts out of an ordered love. How odd it would be to say to another: "I lied to you because I love you." If I really love my friend, I will always act out of honesty. Thus, the orders of love depend upon orders of natural and moral goodness.

I suggest that the fourfold order of goodness in this text can be best understood by means of the musical analogy of a four-note chord. Absolutely speaking, only two notes are required for a chord, since any two notes can form an appropriate relationship of harmony with one another. Thus, the natural and moral goodness unite to form genuine goodness which is harmony. When a third note is added, the intricacy of relationship and the intensity of harmony increases. The act performed out of love has greater intensity of goodness: more depth, more beauty. With the fourth note, the beauty and depth of the chord is enhanced even more. As God's love joins mine, the harmony of goodnesses pour

---

[27] *God and Creatures*, 17.34, p. 398.

forth in exquisite melody. A good act, such as telling the truth, is enhanced with the motivation which stems from right reasoning, further embellished when performed out of love and completely fulfilled when rewarded. Like the wind chime, the perfected act is a delightful combination of beautiful pieces in harmonious relationship with one another.

An especially attractive aspect to Scotus's musical imagery is God's reaction of acceptance. In one text, Scotus describes the divine response to human moral goodness as the delight of a listener to musical harmony. The human eye may be significant for moral judgment, but the divine ear is clearly the image Scotus prefers to express how the moral act relates to God. It is auditory, and not visual, imagery which is used to tie human moral decisions to their foundation in the divine law and to their reward in the divine act of acceptance. The moral person performs for a delighted divine audience of three, continually receiving God's standing ovation.

In *Lectura* I, 17, the image of chords on a harp capture the relationship of internal order with delight in the listener. The harp strings are plucked in a certain order, and this order can admit of harmony or dissonance. When such an order is harmonic, either because a certain string is plucked after another or because the two (or more) strings are struck simultaneously, the sound produces pleasure and delight for those present. The delight is not a function of the individual notes themselves, but rather of their ordered relationship with one another.[28]

In the *Ordinatio* version, this image of the listener delighted by the harmonic chord describes the order of merit and its foundation in divine *acceptatio* or acceptance of human moral actions inspired by love. The divine ear hears the morally good act informed by love and, pleased with its harmony, rewards the act and brings it into the order of merit. The presence of charity within the ordered act resembles harmony within music.

> Likewise, sound comes more from percussion of a sounding body than from the order of percussion and yet, as acceptable to the sense of hearing, it is more from the order of percussion than from the efficacy of the power causing the sound; indeed it is totally

---

[28] *Lectura* I, 17, n. 95 (17:211).

unacceptable to the sense of hearing, if it is not an harmonic sound.[29]

In addition to the use of musical harmony to capture the relationship of the morally good person to God, Scotus uses musical imagery in his discussion of the relation of moral law to fundamental moral principle. In III, 37 the commands of the second table of the Decalogue are said to be in harmony (*consona*) with the first principle of all moral living "God is to be loved."

> The other way in which things belong to the law of nature is because they are exceedingly in harmony (*consona*) with that law, even though they do not follow necessarily from those first practical principles known from their terms, principles which are necessarily grasped by any intellect understanding those terms. Now, it is certain that all the precepts of the second table also belong to the natural law in this way, since their rightness is very much in harmony (*valde consonat*) with the first practical principles that are known of necessity.[30]

The harmonic integrity and coherence of moral principles appear again in IV, 17 where Scotus discusses the relation of positive to natural law.

> As for the supporting argument from reason, I grant that we know by the natural light of the mind that a guilty person must be judged, or at least we recognize that this is highly in accord (*valde consona*) with a proposition that is known in this way. For no sin should be left unpunished anywhere if there is one ruler of the universe and he is just — something which we know naturally or recognize as exceedingly in harmony (*valde consonum*) with what we do know in this way. I even concede further what is said about the necessity of another as judge. But just who is this other? From what is known by natural reason, or from what is consonant (*consona*) with this, such a judge would be God alone, the one who rewards merit and punishes sin.[31]

---

[29] I, 17, n. 152 (5:212).

[30] *Ordinatio* III, suppl. dist. 37, Codex A, in *Will and Morality*, p. 279.

[31] Text established from Codex A in *Will and Morality*, pp. 266-268.

The law as foundation for moral judgment possesses a coherency which resembles musical harmony. Thus, the universe witnesses to the harmonic configuration of the divine musician. Law is neither impersonal nor necessary. On the contrary, it is very personal, highly creative and brilliantly executed by the symphony of nature. The symphony around us provides the basic musical notation for our own moral actions. When we pay attention to and imitate the goodness of nature, we have the foundation for our own creativity: our personal variation on a theme. As moral agents, we participate freely in the cosmic chorus of creativity, harmony and beauty.

The discussion of the sense of hearing is appropriate to the highest level of human rational judgment: an immediate awareness of the truth of a proposition. This appeal to musical imagery appears in *De Primo Principio*, where Scotus discusses the concept *ens infinitum* (infinite being) as the goal of philosophical reflection proper to metaphysics. When the mind arrives at the concept of infinite being, the next natural question is that of its existence, or of the possibility of its existence. In one reflection upon infinite being as possible, Scotus appeals to the absence of dissonance between the term *ens* and the term *infinitum*.

> The intellect, whose object is being, finds nothing repugnant about the notion of something infinite. Indeed, the infinite seems to be the most perfect thing we can know. Now if tonal discord so easily displeases the ear, it would be strange if some intellect did not clearly perceive the contradiction between infinite and its first object [viz. being] if such existed. For if the disagreeable becomes offensive as soon as it is perceived, why is it that no intellect naturally shrinks from infinite being as it would from something out of harmony with, and even destructive of, its first object?[32]

He concludes that there is nothing in the terms themselves which would make them mutually exclusive. Thus *ens infinitum* is possible and, if possible, necessary. Scotus himself calls this passage a *coloratio*, or touching up, of Anselm's argument. To his auditory imagery, Scotus adds a visual emphasis.

All of these passages share a common aesthetic perspective. Whether by auditory or visual imagery, Scotus seeks to describe the activity of rationality as a dynamic and creative process which involves a

---

[32] In *A Treatise on God*, IV, 4.64, pp. 122-123.

search for beauty through different aspects of sense perception. Rational reflection involves not only a trained eye but a trained ear. In addition, the texts from III, 37, IV, 17 and *De Primo Principio* use the auditory image to capture certain and immediate knowledge.

This relationship of the mind to beauty has a long philosophical history. Plato's *Symposium* celebrates the rational search as the ascent to beauty. Augustine echoes the Platonic in his hymn to God as that Beauty he had longed for and finally discovered in his conversion to Christianity (*Confessions* X, 27). The intriguing aspect of Scotus's presentation is the manner in which beauty functions as the focus for both human and divine love. In human choices we seek to love the good, and the morally good act is described as a beautiful whole, a work of art. In Scotus we find as well a description of divine love directed toward human beauty located in the moral choices informed by love. The morally good act and person are embellished by the presence of charity. They are beautiful and loved by God. Scotus's presentation creates a dynamic of divine and human mutuality focused on beauty.

Scotus's early and fundamental rejection of necessary causality and determinism explains his preference for artistic rather than medical imagery. Freedom is definitive of the moral life and suggests an organization of ethical aspects around the will as rational potency. Virtues such as charity embellish the soul with permanence of goodness, but they are not necessary components which can be reduced to learned repetition. The Scotist refusal to consider necessity as part of the moral domain is consistent with the traditional Franciscan preference for the will over the intellect. But it also points to his historical context at the close of the 13th century, in the wake of the Condemnation of 1277.[33] Scotus harmonizes divine and human activity by means of the artistic/aesthetic paradigm, both in his discussion of divine freedom for creation and human freedom for moral goodness. Freedom and creativity become not only expressions of human moral excellence but also exemplify divine activity.

---

[33] For a discussion of the rejection of the necessitarian cosmology of the Arab thinkers and its influence on Scotus's new notion of freedom see Ludger Honnefelder, "Die Kritik des Johannes Duns Scotus am kosmologischen Nezessitarismus der Araber: Ansätze zu einem neuen Freiheitsbegriff" in J. Fried (Hrsg.), *Die abendländische Freiheit vom 10. zum 14. Jahrhundert* (Vorträge und Forschungen 39). Sigmaringen 1991, 249-263.

The rejection of any necessity within the moral realm and defense of freedom is clear throughout Scotus's texts. He begins his *Ordinatio* with a Prologue in which he denies any real knowledge of the ultimate goal of human action, in the absence of Revelation. Against those philosophers who present a "natural goal of human excellence" as necessary result of our natural desire for God, Scotus makes two important points. First, since the activity of human understanding is limited, we can never know with any certainty the reality to which terms such as "human excellence" or "human perfection" refer.[34] Revelation provides specific information which philosophy ought to take seriously. But Revelation cannot be reduced to philosophical reflection upon human nature. If we have a "natural desire," it is one which can only be fulfilled by means of a higher agent. In fact, our realization that we need God to bring us to fulfillment is evidence of our higher understanding; in our weakness is our strength.[35]

Scotus's second point in the Prologue is the denial of any natural necessity in God's relationship to us. God's actions are eminently free and creative, therefore philosophy can provide us with no real information about the goal which awaits human longing.

> But the pilgrim cannot know these [the end, the means or what God will accept] by natural reason. First, since beatitude is conferred as a reward for merit which God accepts as worthy of such reward and consequently it does not follow by natural necessity from any of our acts but contingently given by God, accepting some acts related to himself as meritorious. This is not naturally knowable, as it seems, since here even the philosophers were in error, claiming that all that is from God immediately is necessarily from him.[36]

God's choice to reward human actions extends far beyond the realm of strict justice.[37]

With his rejection of an objective or pre-determined external goal for human moral reflection available to natural reason alone, Scotus

---

[34] *Lectura* Prologue, n. 12 (16:5); *Ordinatio* Prologue, n. 14, (1:10).

[35] *Ordinatio* Prologue n. 75 (1:46).

[36] *Ordinatio* Prologue, n. 18 (1:12).

[37] *Ordinatio* I, 17, n. 149 (5:210-211). Paul Vignaux has devoted much research to this idea of divine liberality in Scotus. See, for example, his "Valeur morale et valeur de salut" in *Homo et Mundus*, Rome 1984, pp. 53-67.

focuses his discussion upon the function of moral living. The object of moral reflection is not, he states, an abstract excellence but the perfection of the human person.[38] Just as the object of medical reflection is not health, but healthy people, so moral philosophy focuses upon the person in her moral functioning. In this light, his choice for the artistic rather than the medical paradigm is significant. The arts, and especially music, provide a better paradigm for the actual functioning internal to an activity rather than for a state to which the artisan aspires. The "state" is in fact nothing more than the best functioning possible.[39] Aristotle himself ends Book VIII of the *Politics* with a reflection upon the education of character, and specifically with the relationship of the study of music to the development of characters capable of "loving and hating rightly."[40]

The concentration on music as related to the divine ear or even as it can be used to describe immediate acts of human rationality points to the importance of music in medieval education. As one of the arts studied in the *quadrivium*, along with mathematics, geometry and astronomy, music held a "scientific" status close to the certainty of mathematics. Augustine's treatise *De Musica* (On Music) affirmed the parallel between the mathematical and musical.[41] Thus, the appreciation of harmony in music was not a matter for personal taste, but a function of the objective proportion between notes and within a chord. Scotus's emphasis upon the aesthetic in a moral discussion is not to be read in light of contemporary theories of art, particularly overly subjective ones. As an art, music held a high status for the medievals based upon the mathematical certainty of proportions. This type of certainty appropriately grounds moral principles, not as the result of divine whim, but as ordered and rational manifestations of the relationships within reality, founded upon the divine will. For the purposes of Scotus's discussion,

[38] *Ordinatio* Prologue Pars 5, q. 1-2, n. 262 (1:177).

[39] See *Nicomachean Ethics* Book I, 1097b25, where Aristotle refers to the notion of the highest good in terms of functioning.

[40] "Since then music is a pleasure, and excellence consists in rejoicing and loving and hating rightly, there is clearly nothing which we are so much concerned to acquire and to cultivate as the power of forming right judgments and of taking delight in good dispositions and noble actions." *Politics*, Book VIII, 5 (1340a14-19). Later, Aristotle expressly states that music has the "power to form character" (1340b11).

[41] Henry Chadwick, *Augustine*, Oxford University Press 1986 (Past Masters), pp. 44-48.

music offers the model of an art which embraces both objective certainty and subjective taste. It is, then, a more significant example of the reasoning proper to moral agency than is medicine.

Conclusion

Scotus's discussion of moral goodness and its relationship to God offers a better context for his moral insights than the discussion of freedom in chapter two. While the possibility for free choice is *sine qua non* for any moral discussion, the quality of moral actions represents a more significant content for discussion. To be sure, the affection for justice is the rational dimension which has access to moral principles, such as the first command to love God. But, in addition, Scotus's presentation of moral goodness as an artistic act personalizes his discussion of the ethical realm and links it to God as divine artist and lawgiver. This enhanced personalization results in a perspective which focuses on love and relationship as central to moral living. In addition, several aspects emerge as significant contributions to moral discourse.

First, if we consider both the auditory and visual motifs in light of the discussion of moral decision-making and action, we discover a perspective which offers the best of both the virtue-based and principle-based in contemporary discourse. The issue of character involves internal integrity and coherence between principles and values. This integrity is a *consona* or harmony which develops between first practical principles and lesser principles derived from them. The harmony here is expressed as musicality where notes form fuller and fuller chords as they are in an ordered relationship to one another. The musical analogy informs a reading of Quodlibet Question 17 where Scotus describes the four levels of goodness: objective, moral, charitable and meritorious. Like a four note chord, the meritorious act has a fullness of beauty not found in the earlier chords. Its integrity and harmony delight the divine ear.

Such an artistic framework addresses as well the intricacy at the heart of the virtue/principle moral dynamic. Learned behavior does form character. Principles do form a coherent and integrated whole in a morally mature agent. The domain of human *praxis* includes internal and external realms which are not opposed to one another. Together they form that harmonious unity of character called integrity.

Second, external actions have a relationship to internal principles and values. While this could be termed *consona,* Scotus prefers to use the term "conformity," both to indicate the priority of principle over judgment and to provide for the possibility that one might choose to act counter to the judgment of right reasoning. The moral decision or act of choice involves both internal consonance and external conformity: both auditory and visual beauty. Like the wind chime, moral living is balanced, beautiful and harmonious. Like the artisan, the moral agent works with the material at hand. To whatever imperfect conditions she must bring all the skill of a lifetime of training and attention to the demands of a particular set of circumstances. This attention belongs to the virtue of prudence which has immediate grasp of the particulars in any situation and whose judgment fulfills and perfects principle. The most basic and fundamental dimension of moral principle is embodied in the Decalogue, which both guides and informs the development of moral integrity.

Third, the artistic imagery supports the focus on love and beauty, both in the human moral choices and in the order of divine *acceptatio.* In Scotist thought we discover what has been called the "lost transcendental," beauty, elevated to significance within moral discussion. The native freedom of the human will moves toward the good and seeks to love appropriately. The affection for justice finds its object in *bonum honestum,* or the good of value. For Alexander of Hales, *bonum honestum* was synonymous with beauty.[42] The divine response of acceptance creates the order of merit and crowns the moral act with an added beauty of relationship to God's will.

This imagery integrates the notion of *praxis* around the functioning moral agent. Like the artist or musician, the moral person follows a high standard. Yet the actions of a moral expert are not different in kind from those of any moral agent. Proper and appropriate moral decision-making is itself the goal of human action. It is not simply a question of choosing, but of choosing well and "rejoicing, loving and hating rightly" (Aristotle, *Politics*1340a15).

Finally, Scotus's presentation underscores the personal and relational aspects of moral living. It emphasizes goodness to be enhanced by the operation of human reasoning. Goodness is an intricate and harmonious relationship among several aspects or dimensions within any act:

[42] *Summa Theologica* I, n. 103; t. I, 162. Taken from Allan B. Wolter, OFM, *The Transcendentals and Their Function in the Metaphysics of Duns Scotus,* Franciscan Institute: 1946, p. 100, note 1.

the person, the intention, the act, the time, place and manner. These are all to be balanced according to fundamental principles of love as the binding force among persons. The relationships among all aspects within the moral dynamic produce a moral paradigm which points beyond itself to transcendence and relationship with God. The centrality of love for God and love for neighbor focuses the moral question around human responses to real situations in light of the Gospel. This is a person-centered, not principle-centered moral vision, where the absolute demands of norms may not always be realized. In such cases, the possibility for moral goodness still exists. The ability to make moral decisions in difficult circumstances comes as a result of moral training and experience. Drawn toward beauty, the moral person seeks to enhance both beauty of character and beauty of action. The central moral imperatives of love for God and neighbor are both accessible to natural reasoning and available to the will through the affection for justice. Proper reflection on the significant aspects of human nature, such as intellection and love, reveal those actions which promote fundamental human goods. These goods are not limited to the Christian tradition but belong to all persons of good will: truth, peace and harmony.[43]

Thus, Scotus's discussion might not represent a better use of Aristotle than that found in Aquinas, nor even a use which is incompatible with a Thomasian interpretation of moral living. Rather, Scotus offers a vision of the moral domain which emphasizes love at its center and creativity as the fullest expression of moral excellence. In addition, his perspective focuses on the activity itself and tightens the link between functioning and goal. Each action is not seen as means to a future goal, but as the goal-in-becoming. An artistic model may provide a better integration of means and end, one where a disjunction is less likely to occur than in a medical perspective.

Scotus's predilection for the artistic and musical imagery in his thinking may indicate a richness in his thought which has not been adequately treated or appreciated, beyond the 1972 article by Francis Kovach, "Divine and Human Beauty in the Philosophy and Theology of

[43] This position is similar to that of Germain Grisez who states, "Since human goodness is found in the fullness of human being, one begins to understand what it is to be a good person by considering what things fulfill human persons. Things which do so are human goods in the central sense — that is, intelligible goods." He identifies harmony as a "reflexive good", that is, one which includes choice in its definition. See *The Way of the Lord Jesus*, Franciscan Herald Press 1983, vol. I, pp. 121-125.

Scotus."[44] This imagery brings together the artistic and the ethical in a way not found in Aquinas. Scotus emphasizes the value of beauty for moral action and the attractiveness of the beautiful as moral motivation, thus touching into one of the ancient meanings of *to ethos* which linked character to art.[45]

The development of this aesthetic imagery is founded upon the rejection of the necessary and the presentation of freedom as creative expression of the human relationship to God. In ethical living, each person is an artisan of character and beautiful action. Moral living, then, belongs to a broader domain of spirituality and participation in the life of God. The specifically musical quality of Scotus's perspective enables him to deal with the elements of intensity and immediacy of judgment as belonging to the moral expert. The notion of the harmonic chord illustrates the coherence and integrity of the moral life. The Decalogue provides the dimension of objectivity and rectitude. Finally, at the highest level of goodness within human action, we become co-creators and co-artists, co-musicians with God, whose ear is delicately attuned to the music of the human heart.

[44] In this article, Kovach examines the transcendentality of beauty for Scotus and considers the objectivity of the aesthetic judgment, calling him an "aesthetic objectivist".

[45] Cf. *Oxford English Dictionary*, 314: Ethos: "In reference to ancient aesthetic criticism and rhetoric. Aristotle's statement that Polygnotus excelled all other painters in the representation of *ethos* apparently meant simply that his pictures expressed "character"; but as Aristotle elsewhere says that this painter portrayed men as nobler than they really are, some modern writers have taken *ethos* to mean "ideal excellence".

four

Virtue: Integrity *of* Character

In 1981 Alasdaire MacIntyre revitalized moral discussion with his
insightful work, *After Virtue.*[1] MacIntyre explains contemporary
moral fragmentation in light of a loss of virtue, that is, a lost understanding of the nature and function of virtue and the virtues in moral
living. Not only is there a general failure to understand correctly the
notion of virtue for classical writers, but there is as yet no coherent
moral model which integrates virtue into contemporary discussion. The
task for moral theorists today, he argues, is the rediscovery of the virtue
tradition as a superior moral paradigm. The years since 1981 have seen
increased interest and discussion of the nature of virtue, of its role in
moral living and of its influence on moral character.

The preceding chapters have focused upon the relational aspect
within moral living: person in communion, freedom for values, goodness as beauty. All three have emphasized freedom as key to the moral
discussion. This raises the following questions: what value, if any, do the
virtues hold for Scotus? If virtue is learned behavior, then is character
simply the result of a good moral environment? What is the relationship
of freedom to virtue? Is freedom the only moral value for Scotus, or are
there other, habitual elements in moral living which promote beauty
and goodness? In other words, how does Scotus affirm both the value of
freedom and the importance of virtue in moral living?

Scotus's moral discussion affirms both the centrality of freedom
and the importance of natural gifts and virtues. The relationship of

[1]   Notre Dame Press 1981, 1986.

freedom and virtue exhibits that mutuality which is within the human heart; we are both naturally and freely drawn toward what we perceive to be good. For Scotus, the virtues represent natural dispositions toward good actions which never replace free choice. In fact, they are themselves generated by acts of choice within the will and are perfected through repetition. Virtues fall into two categories: theological (faith, hope and charity) and moral (justice, fortitude and temperance). The virtue of right reasoning, prudence, governs the moral virtues within the will, but is itself located in the intellect. Like his discussion of moral goodness, Scotus's teaching on virtue reveals a harmony among several dimensions: the natural (insofar as virtues are dispositions in the will), the moral (insofar as they are the product of choice and governed by prudence), the intellectual (insofar as prudence unifies and directs virtues) and the theological (insofar as some virtues are infused by grace). Together these dimensions constitute moral character and unify acts of choice, situating both within the context of goodness which is broader than the will's capacity for free choice and richer than the goodness of any one act of right choosing. The realm of virtue underpins the workings of free choice: the virtues enhance the operation of the free and rational will. This enhancement is double: intentionally and extensionally. Intentionally, virtues strengthen the relationship of right reasoning to the good, enabling the will to choose the good with ease. Extensionally, the virtues support the establishment of character throughout a lifetime.

The relation of virtues to the will resembles the organization of pieces in the wind chime to its center. There can be any number of pieces. They can be large or small. Their material could be metal, wood or ceramic. The presence of the pieces around the disk is required for the music; their number, size and material determine what sort of sound the chime produces. Larger, stronger pieces are needed for a deep, rich tone. Smaller pieces balance these with lighter, more delicate sound. Not every chime has the same pieces. Likewise, not everyone possesses the same natural virtues, yet everyone has at least a few inclinations toward goodness. Like the pieces, virtues surround the moral centerpiece (the will) and help to constitute the harmony of character.

It is important to note at this point that Scotus's treatment of virtue is not central to his moral discussion. It follows from his emphasis on the freedom within the will as primary moral element. He attempts, nonetheless, to integrate the discussion of virtue within his larger consideration of the will. As such, he does not focus on a separation of moral from theological virtues, but rather analyzes how any virtue, as *habitus*[2] (practical habit), influences free choice. Scotus turns readily to a causal examination of the way natural inclination participates in moral action and enhances the morally good act. In other words, he treats practical habits as causes for moral action. They are important but not as essential as freedom in the will. Since freedom defines the moral realm, it is the primary cause for any moral act. There are, however, secondary causes which contribute to moral action and which influence the operation of the will. These are the virtues, the practical habits which constitute character.

Scotus's desire to integrate virtue into his discussion of free choice points to his vision of moral living which balances natural gifts and talents with freedom and rationality. This is indeed an "anthropocentric perspective" which focuses on natural human goodness and potential for right action. The natural capacity for moral action lies both in the constitution of the will (the affection for justice) and in the human orientation toward goodness. Here again, the 12th century moral discussion[3] provides elements for Scotus which he integrates with the Aristotelian insights regarding *praxis* as a dynamic activity of the will which cannot be discussed apart from moral inclinations.

---

[2] The Latin *habitus* is difficult to translate into English. It does not correspond to the word "habit", but rather to the notion of an acquired or learned disposition, tendency or inclination. *Habitus* is the result of training, and the professional tennis player would be said to possess the *habitus* of tennis, just as the artisan or musician would possess their respective *habitus*. For this discussion, I translate it as practical habit, since it refers to a wider spectrum than the narrow, modern notion of virtue.

[3] Cary J. Nederman's article "Nature, Ethics and the Doctrine of *Habitus*: Aristotelian Moral Psychology in the Twelfth Century" (*Traditio* 45 (1989-90), pp.87-110) argues for the development of an "anthropocentric perspective on moral theory" during the 12th century, based upon the notion of *habitus* found in Aristotle's *Categories*. This perspective did not separate the natural from supernatural, but worked to distinguish "the specifically acquired features unique to moral character from all qualities outside of human control — those stemming from an innate or otherwise natural source, as well as from supernatural infusion." (p. 88). Scotus's discussion at the end of the 13th century will go even further to harmonize nature and grace by separating any *habitus* from the free exercise of willing.

The Medieval Discussion of Virtue

We can look upon the formulation of Scotus's position on virtue from two vantage points. First, the place of virtue within medieval moral discussion owes a great deal to the reception of Aristotle's *Nicomachean Ethics* in the 13th century. In this text, the virtues, both moral and intellectual, are intimately related to the realization of the ultimate human goal: they form the core of the Stagirite's theory. Virtues function as those qualities of life related to and constitutive of human fulfillment and happiness. Aristotle's thinking on virtue entered into the medieval context formed by St. Augustine, in whose tradition all Schoolmen wrote. For Augustine, virtue is the proper use of what could be abused;[4] it is the correct ordering of love.[5]

But the Aristotelian discussion is only one dimension. The second vantage point from which to understand the medieval discussion of virtue is that of the 12th century. This tradition appealed to Aristotelian notions found in the *Categories* and *Topics.*[6] Abelard had focused on the development of character and the importance of virtue as "a quality which does not inhere naturally in a thing, but is acquired through careful study or deliberation and is difficult to change."[7] In the final decades of the 12th century, the doctrine of practical habit developed into a deeper moral theory of virtues and vices. Alan of Lille and Simon of Tournai distinguished ordinary dispositions from practical habits by means of "efficacious perseverance" and constancy.[8] In other words, ordinary dispositions could be likened to intentions. The intention to act "is not a sufficient criterion for the possession of a *habitus* (and thus a moral quality)."[9] One only becomes moral by acting in a manner appropriate to the moral person. Character results from conscious choice and action. The notion of practical habit enabled the 12th century discussion to focus on the natural capacity of human persons to acquire moral character through the exercise of moral reasoning and action. This discussion was to be integrated within a renewed under-

---

[4] *De Libero Arbitrio* 2.19.50.

[5] *De Quantitate Animae* 16.27 (PL 32, 1050).

[6] Both available to the Latins since the 5th century.

[7] *Dialogue between a Philosopher, a Jew and a Christian*, Stuttgart 1970, 1988 cited in Cary J. Nederman "Nature, Ethics...", p. 96.

[8] Alan of Lille, *Tractatus de virtutibus et de vitiis et de donis Spiritus Sancti*, 49. In Nederman, "Nature, Ethics...", p. 104.

[9] Nederman, "Nature, Ethics...", p. 104.

standing of key ethical concepts when the entire text of the *Nicomachean Ethics* was made available in the 1250's.

Prior to 1246, when Robert Grosseteste produced a complete translation of the *Ethics*, only books I-III were available. The earliest translation (*Ethica vetus*) appeared in the 12th century and contained Books II and III only. In the first years of the 13th century, another translation appeared of which only Book I (*Ethica nova*) circulated. What happened to the remaining books is unknown. The last important translation appeared between 1260 and 1280, when William of Moerbeke translated the entire work from the original Greek.[10]

During the early years of study on Aristotle's *Nicomachean Ethics* (prior to 1246), most commentators struggled with a correct interpretation of the notions of happiness (*eudaimonia*) and virtue (*arete*), as well as their mutual relationship. To the already difficult pace of the translation and introduction of the text itself, we must add the influence of Stoic thinkers and the importance of the cardinal virtues for late antiquity, coupled with the writings of Greek theologians (Macrobius and John Damascene). All of these factors contributed to an ambiguous, muddied interpretation of Aristotle's ethical concerns,[11] which would not be clarified before the end of the 13th century.

For the medievals, the reception of Aristotle's *Ethics* marked an intellectual turning point of critical magnitude. The historical circumstances under which the text entered the 13th century were paralleled by a gradual appreciation for and understanding of the ethical theory itself and of its implications for Christian moral philosophy. The later years of the century saw a consciousness raising on the part of many theologians: the philosophical import of *eudaimonia* threatened the primacy of theology because it argued for an autonomous philosophical ethics.[12] Gradually, benign interpretations of Aristotle's text prior to 1250 (such as those of Roger Bacon and Albert the Great) gave way to the rad-

---

[10]　Bernard G. Dod, "Aristoteles latinus" in *The Cambridge History of Later Medieval Philosophy,* Kretzmann, Kenny, Pinborg (ed.), Cambridge University Press 1982, pp. 49-50.

[11]　On this, see Georg Wieland's masterful treatment of the development of ethical concerns in early commentaries on *Ethica nova et vetus* in *Ethica: scientia practica,* Münster: Aschendorff 1981.

[12]　For a clear presentation of the historical situation and the introduction of Aristotle's *Ethics,* see G. Wieland, "The Reception of Aristotle's Ethics" in *The Cambridge History...,* pp. 657-672.

ical Aristotelian positions of Siger of Brabant and Boethius of Dacia. These Masters no longer sought to harmonize Aristotle with Christian doctrine: they took the Philosopher at his word and concluded that philosophy alone could indeed lead to the perfectly happy human life. Philosophical teachings such as this within the Faculty of Arts threatened the primacy of theology for practical questions. As Georg Wieland so clearly documents,[13] the crisis surrounded the concept of *beatitude* and the innate human capacity for moral excellence. The response of theologians to this new form of philosophical Pelagianism was forceful and decisive: the Condemnation of 1277 listed no fewer than 219 philosophical propositions as heterodox.

In his treatment of virtue, Scotus demonstrates at once his keen understanding of Aristotle and, following Augustine, a profound awareness of the human orientation toward grace. He follows William of Ware in an emphasis on freedom in the will as central moral element and integrates the philosophical-theological debate around the notion of virtue as *natural* inclination whose imprint on the soul disposes but does not determine one toward right action. In addition, his treatment of prudence as unifying moral virtue reveals his understanding of the dynamic excellence which belongs to the will in the act of moral deliberation and choice. Such attention to deliberative excellence widens his discussion of virtue beyond the 12th century perspective to include the activity of choice as an "efficacious volition" proper to *praxis.* It is the rational activity of the will, and not natural inclinations, which constitutes moral excellence (*arete*). Scotus's texts clearly place moral inclinations within the will and subject to the will's free choice. In addition, they emphasize the very exercise of willing as native to the will and, thus, as constitutive of the means by which the will is perfected.

The Virtues in the Will

Scotus's discussion of virtue as natural disposition never threatens the primacy of freedom within the will. In III, suppl. D. 33 he states that both the will and the intellect are capable of performing acts which are morally good and correct without the presence of any practical habit, moral or intellectual:

[13]   "Happiness: the perfection of man" in *The Cambridge History...,* pp. 673-686.

One could say to the question [of the will as seat of the moral virtues] that the will on its own without a practical habit could perform an act that is right and morally good — nor is this true only of the will, for the intellect also could perform a correct judgment without an intellectual habit; for the first act of a correct intellect and a will that is right precedes the practical habit in whatsoever degree such exists, for from such acts is generated whatever is first present in a habit. Nevertheless, just as in the intellect, either through its first act or through frequently elicited acts, the habit of prudence is generated, so also with the first correct choice consonant with the dictates of right reason, or through many such correct choices, there is generated in the will a proper virtue which inclines the will to choose rightly.[14]

In this passage, Scotus grounds the independence of the will and the intellect on the fact that the practical habit itself must be generated by the faculty involved. This means that right choice in the will generates the practical habit called moral virtue, just as right judgment in the intellect generates the virtue of prudence. The first act of the will, free choice, precedes the virtues and is the source for the development of any practical habit which assists the will in subsequent moral deliberation. Thus, no virtue need exist for the will to choose rightly. If it were necessary, then how could anyone explain the first act of choice which generated the practical habit? Virtue must follow the act of right choosing.

Later in this question, Scotus recalls the 12th century distinction to emphasize that it is the act of choice and not mere volition which is the source for moral virtue.

Hence one could say that in those who have a sensitive appetite, the will could be a principle of many choices in regard to moral good, and this efficacious volition is what we call "choosing." This alone is suited by nature to produce the sort of practical habit which, though prior to any practical habit in the sense appetite, is nevertheless suited to be a principle for commanding such an appetite.[15]

This dense passage offers an excellent example of the close workings of natural inclinations and free choice. Sense perceptions provide the

---

[14]   *Will and Morality,* p. 333.
[15]   *Will and Morality,* p. 339.

rational will with options for actions. These options come from external stimuli as well as internal powers such as imagination and memory. This means that, in any choice, I am confronted with what lies before me as well as any information I bring from my past: memories of similar choices. Knowing "what to look for" in a situation is developed over time and only by means of moments of choice. If I have learned from past mistakes I'll know what to avoid, what to promote. This deeper moral knowledge commands sense perception, since it directs my vision (for example) to seek out and identify significant data for the moral choice. But this deeper moral knowledge only develops through correct identification of significant moral data. In other words, right choosing produces moral expertise.

The distinction between volition and choice points to the existence of natural inclinations toward rational action over which the will has control. Scotus only considers these virtues when they actually participate in moral choice. For instance, I may be a very imaginative person, but my tendency toward creative scenario may not always enter into an actual decision. When it does, my imagination becomes a real moral virtue. When it does not, it is merely a practical inclination which might be of use to me. Knowing when to use my imagination and when not to, however, is an important virtue and one which governs whatever use I make of my imaginative gifts. For Scotus, any inclination which is not directly related to the act of choosing rightly is not a virtue in the proper sense. The wider sort of inclination resides in the sense appetite, not the rational will:

> One can concede, however, that if the will by willing can command the sense appetite (by moderating either its passion or the way it goes after or flees from a thing, if this be an act of the sense appetite), it can also leave behind in the sense appetite by such correct commands some practical habit that inclines that appetite to move more readily towards sensibles in the way the will commands. And this practical habit that is left there, although it is not properly a virtue, because it is not an elective habit, nor does it incline one to make choices, can in some sense be conceded to be a virtue, since it inclines one to such things as are in accord with right reason.[16]

---

[16] *Will and Morality,* p. 335.

My will is entirely responsible for my moral development, as we see in this passage. It is my will which commands proper use of my senses and sense appetite. So I command proper use of my imagination and can oversee within it the development of rational tendencies which facilitate its proper use. The activity of problem-solving, for example, uses the imagination in a specific manner. Here the imagination does not just come up with any alternative scenario, but with specific scenario which are appropriate to the case at hand. Someone trained in problem-solving moves more quickly to find creative solutions than does someone who has not had much experience with this activity. Both persons may have the same degree of imagination. Scotus would say the first person retains the practical habit of problem-solving which, while not technically a virtue, does assist in virtuous action.

Such inclinations contribute indirectly to moral choice and belong to a wider understanding of virtue. The narrower sense of virtue for Scotus applies only to those practical habits developed through my acts of deliberation and choice which themselves incline me to choose correctly.

> Also, the will first wills something in itself before it commands any act of an inferior potency in regard to such, for it is not because it commands the inferior potency that it wills such a thing, but vice versa. Therefore, in that prior state, the will by its right choices — since it is just as indeterminate and able to be determined as is the intellect — generates in itself a practical habit inclining it to choose rightly, and this will most properly be called a virtue, because it is the elective habit that most properly inclines the will to act in the way it was generated, by making right choices.[17]

Moral virtues belong to the will in its activity of deliberation and choice. They are generated within the will and incline the will toward habitual repetition of the correct operation. The key distinction between virtues in the sense appetite and in the rational will reveals Scotus's effort to distance himself slightly from the 12th century discussion of *habitus*, affirm the freedom of the will and nonetheless affirm the existence of virtue in the will which is more than just natural inclination.

A reprise of an earlier example may help to clarify this distinction. In chapter two, I referred to an exercise of deliberation involving the

---

17   *Will and Morality,* p. 333.

alternatives of working in the garden, working on a chapter or reading
a book. A fourth alternative which emerged from that discussion was
the choice to do nothing at all. For present purposes, I exclude this last
alternative here. Scotus mentions two sorts of inclinations which can be
called virtue: a broader set not directly related to choice and a more narrow set immediately involved in the activity of practical reasoning.[18] In
the case of this example, I could name certain inclinations toward
learning, toward finishing a project or toward tending the garden.
These might influence my final decision but do not enter directly into
the deliberative process. Their influence could be limited to those
aspects which I allow to influence my decision about what to do with my
time.

Other, more significant inclinations deal directly with the activity
of deliberation and choice: proper consideration of consequences of
each course of action, awareness of time constraints or deadlines, any
relevant promises, self-control, the ability to follow through on decisions, etc. These inclinations are generated in the activity of decision-
making and facilitate subsequent decisions in a more direct manner
than those mentioned above. Such *praxis*-specific inclinations would
qualify for the narrow understanding of virtue. They do not determine
the outcome, but they offer influences which speed up the process.

Scotus affirms the close link between virtuous dispositions and the
will when he identifies "acting virtuously" with "acting with deliberation."

> No virtue acts with absolutely no deliberation. For just as no one
> acts in a fully human way unless that person acts intelligently, so —
> as regards those things that pertain to the end — no one acts in a
> human fashion without understanding the reason for acting, and
> this understanding is what deliberation means. Hence no one acts
> virtuously by acting suddenly without deliberation in the way
> nature acts according to II *Physics*.[19]

At issue here is the notion of *natural* virtue and how it relates to the
operation of freely willing what is good. Virtue cannot be *natural* if this
means *necessary*, that is, according to a natural, predictable causality

---

[18] Aristotle also distinguishes moral characteristics from intellectual excellence
needed for deliberation. See *Nicomachean Ethics* VI,1 (1138b35-1139a16).
[19] *Will and Morality*, p. 345.

("the way nature acts"). Virtue is *natural* (native) however insofar as it belongs to the nature of the will (as free cause) to generate acts of deliberation and choice which leave their imprint upon the soul. These imprints enable the will to act more easily within subsequent opportunities for reasoning and choice. This ease appears clearly, states Scotus, in the rapidity with which some mature moral agents are capable of coming to a moral judgment.

> Hence, the dictum of the Philosopher should be understood in this way. Just as the virtuous person is inclined to choose rightly by reason of a correct practical habit, so too he has been conditioned by prudence to make at once a correct judgment as to what should be chosen, and to deliberate imperceptibly, as it were, because of the rapidity with which the practical inference is made. Another, imperfect individual, however, syllogizes practically only with difficulty and delay. And if at last he chooses correctly, he is said to act not suddenly but sullenly, whereas another, perfect person as it were acts quickly with respect to that thing, since the time it takes him to act is imperceptibly short.[20]

Virtue deals with the activity within the will and directly influences the rapidity with which the moral agent is able to come to a decision and act. Scotus situates the discussion of virtue at a level internal to the will and to the activity of moral deliberation and choice. Virtue is not identified with external behavior but with dispositions of character which enable me to arrive quickly at a moral judgment and follow it through to choice and execution.

Because of the centrality of freedom for his moral perspective, Scotus separates the notion of virtue as natural inclination from that of the moral dispositions within the will which relate directly to the exercise of deliberation and choice. These constitute the moral character of an individual. The actual operation of decision making and choice unifies moral living around the will. This operation involves virtues, yet not in a way which compromises the will's innate freedom for self-determination.

---

[20] *Will and Morality*, pp. 345-7.

84

 THE HARMONY OF GOODNESS

Virtue and Moral Action

As we have seen, virtue is learned behavior but does not influence the moral realm in any kind of determining sense. This means that, no matter how much training I have had in making right decisions, I cannot guarantee that I will always decide rightly. This is because my freedom takes precedence over my qualities of character. Scotus explains this by means of a causal discussion, where he likens the virtues to partial causes which bring their influence to bear on moments of choice. Because they are partial, they never entirely determine the outcome. They fall under the direction of the rational will, which is the higher, directing cause.

There are two passages where Scotus explains the relationship of two causes working together. The first is from *Additiones* II, 25 [21] where he speaks of "partial co-causality" in terms of the father and mother for the birth of a child. One cause is the principal agent for the resulting effect and the other the lesser cause, but both function together as one total cause.[22]

The second passage makes much more of partial co-causality in terms of the virtuous life. In *Ordinatio* I, 17 Scotus deals with the question of exactly how any practical habit (or virtue) affects moral goodness. He begins the discussion with a reminder that goodness is like beauty: the harmonic configuration of all aspects of an act. So where is virtue to be found?

This question brings out the philosophical issue at stake for any ethical theory. For Aristotle's *Nicomachean Ethics*, the goal of human living is the development of a *second nature* for goodness: the moral expert acts well naturally, just as the athlete consistently performs at a high level of perfection. The good person can be counted on to make excellent moral choices quickly. While Scotus accepts the possibility of moral development, he hesitates to accept this sort of *second nature* as realizable. Here it is important to remember just what the word *natural* means for Scotus. Nature acts in a predictable manner, therefore the term *natural* brings with it connotations of necessity and determinism.

---

[21] Later additions to *Ordinatio* provided by William of Alnwick. The text for this was originally published by Charles Balic as "Une question inédite de J. Duns Scot sur la volonté" in *Recherches de Théologie ancienne et médiévale* 3 (1931) 198-208.
[22] "Une question...", p. 203.

These connotations run counter to Scotus's affirmation of human freedom. He never affirms that moral living becomes *second nature*.

When Scotus deals with the question of the role of virtue in I, 17 he begins by clarifying that no natural inclination nor practical habit can replace the importance of free choice within the will. But this is not to say that virtue is insignificant for moral living. In fact, an act performed solely on the part of the will and with no practical habit involved is less perfect than the same act performed with the will and virtue in collaboration.

When both the will and virtue are present, the will functions according to both free and natural dimensions. This is the fullness of moral excellence: the moral act has greater intensity than the same act performed solely by the will. For instance, a freely chosen act of generosity is most intense when the practical habit for generosity is also present. This does not mean that a generous act which might "go against the grain" of my normal pattern is not morally good. A morally good act may indeed spring from the will alone, but in such a case this act would simply be less perfect than one which results from the free and natural causes working in tandem. The perfect moral act is born from the interaction of freedom and natural inclination, much the same way that a child is born from both parents.

> However, it [the will] works less perfectly without the practical habit than with it (and this granting equal effort on the part of the will) just as when two causes concur toward one effect, one alone cannot by itself [cause] the effect as perfectly as the two can together. In this way the position is saved whereby the act has greater intensity when it comes from the will and practical habit than from the will alone... because two concurrent causes can produce a more perfect effect than either one alone, — which effect however is itself a whole and "per se" one from two causes, but in diverse causal relations.[23]

Even though the perfect moral act is related to both the natural and free dimensions of human action, these relationships are not equal. The free dimension is obviously the more important, since free choice does in fact define the moral realm as "voluntary." This co-causal relationship between freedom and moral virtue is a type of mutuality which we saw

[23] I, 17, n. 40 (5:154).

earlier in the discussion of the essential order.[24] Both freedom and natural inclination are equally related to the perfect moral act. They are not, however, equal in their importance for the moral act. One need only reflect upon an act performed without thinking to realize that natural inclinations or virtues do not totally explain moral perfection.

An example here, taken from another Scotist text, may help us. Suppose one were walking down the street and encountered a beggar. The act of almsgiving is a laudatory one, and could be an example of the morally good act. The act, however, could be performed from any one of a number of motives. If the act came simply from the natural or unconscious habitual disposition of giving generously, then it would not be considered moral, nor would we want to praise someone for such an unconscious act, no matter how good it is. The same act, done from free choice and as a result of conscious reflection, would be morally good or virtuous, since it would be both in the control of the agent's will and done according to rational reflection.[25] In addition, if this deliberation and choice were accompanied by an habitual inclination toward generosity, it would have even richer goodness. For one thing, it would be easier to accomplish and produce joy. The free choice to give alms to the beggar is intensified by the natural disposition to love others. Specifically, this means that the mature moral agent would perform the generous act more quickly than would the person without such moral maturity.

For Scotus, moral living has both free and natural components. The free component is within the will as rational and capable of self-control. The natural component involves learned, habitual inclinations which are also within the will as it is drawn toward the good. In moral development, free and natural elements enter into a closer working relationship, a type of marriage which gives birth to perfect moral actions. For the person who is morally mature, the "expert," these dimensions constitute the integrity of character.

[24] See chapter 1, pp. 17-18.
[25] See Scotus's treatment of this example in II, 7, nn. 28-30. An English excerpt of this distinction (nn. 28-39) is found in *Will and Morality*, pp. 218-225. In this text, Scotus refers to a four-fold goodness: the first level of natural goodness and three levels of moral goodness: virtuous or circumstantial, meritorious or gratuitous, and the act as accepted and rewarded by God.

Prudence and Moral Virtue

A third aspect of character involves the rationality of the will. In chapter two, we saw this was synonymous with the affection for justice: it expresses itself in self-control. The practical habit which is associated with this quality is prudence, or right reasoning. Unlike the other moral virtues, prudence lies in the intellect and not in the will. It governs the development of virtues in the will because it offers the will the help of reason. The will is rational, states Scotus, because it uses the intellect.

Of all the dimensions of character, this is perhaps the most important for Scotus. It is in the relationship of prudence and moral virtue that he locates the most serious potential for error, for moral fragmentation. Even though the will is rational and capable of coming to a conclusion about what ought to be done, this process of reflection does not guarantee moral action. Despite its rationality, the will always retains the freedom to act otherwise than reason commands, or to refrain from acting altogether.

Of course, this is not the only area where moral error is possible. As we have seen, there are numerous opportunities for moral fragmentation; developing the appropriate inclinations into practical habits so that they might function as moral virtues is in itself an arduous task. But as the process of moral integration continues, we become aware that perfect moral action can never be guaranteed. This awareness comes from an experience of freedom which never leaves our moral consciousness.

The centrality of freedom in Scotist thought affects the relationship between prudence and moral virtue. For Scotus, it is possible to have a correct judgment about what ought to be done without any moral virtue in the will. This means quite simply that, not only is the rational will powerful enough to know what to do in the absence of natural inclination, but it is also free enough to know what to do and do nothing at all.

This type of freedom is a form of self-control: it reveals itself in the rational ability to "hold back" from an action. It is the interaction of the two affections in the will. Normally this sort of self-control is morally appropriate. One needs to think twice before acting. However, it is possible that such self-restraint can impede moral progress. If I hesitate too often, I may never perform a moral act. This is, of course, an extreme scenario, but it explains well the heart of moral freedom for Scotus. It also links the notion of freedom with that of virtue in the will. Augustine had defined virtue as "the right use of what could be abused."[26] For Scotus, the freedom of the will lies in its control over itself. This control is also rational. It can be misused if it interferes with right action following upon right deliberation. In other words, for Scotus, our greatest gift (rational freedom) can be misused and become our greatest liability.

As a free potency, the will is capable of self-determined choice, involving both objects external to itself and its own internal acts. At a primary level, the will can freely choose (*velle*) or reject (*nolle*) an object. At a deeper level, however, the will can choose to refrain from choice (*non velle*). Scotus's discussion of prudence is best understood in light of the rationality of the affection for justice and the freedom of *non velle*. In the Prologue to the *Lectura* and *Ordinatio*, Scotus defines the domain of *praxis* and its relationship to practical wisdom. The *Ordinatio* discussion defines *praxis* as "the elicited act of the will" even when not accompanied by the commanded act of execution.[27] The elicited act of the will can apply either to an external object or to the act of willing itself. Scotus states, for example, that "...in regard to any object, then, the will is able not to will or nill it, and *can suspend itself from eliciting any act in particular with regard to this or that.*" (emphasis mine)[28] This is an act which anyone can experience through introspection. This is an act of "turning away" from choice. This act applies to the act of willing itself. One can affirm then, that the will's power extends both to objects outside itself and to its own act. This is the power for self-restraint discussed previously. Scotus's discussion of prudence refers to this internal act as well as that of the will which, as in texts of Thomas Aquinas, considers external objects functioning as means to a pre-determined end. Thus Scotus broadens his discussion of prudence to include internal self-restraint as well as acts of choice involving objects external to the will.

As the internal act, *praxis* functions as the object of the practical habit, particularly the practical intellect. Since the nature of the object defines the nature of the practical habit, the practical intellect requires an object which belongs to the domain of *praxis*. The act of choice, considered in itself as commanded by the will, belongs most perfectly to the domain of *praxis* and is the most perfect object of any practical habit. Thus, while the practical intellect can consider objects external to the

---

[26]   See note 4 above.

[27]   *Ordinatio* Prologue Pars 5, q. 1-2, n. 314 (1:207).

[28]   *Ordinatio* IV, suppl. d. 49 qq. 9-10, Codex A f 282va, in *Will and Morality*, p. 195.

will, a far superior activity would be the consideration of the act of will-ing itself in its perfection as free and rational.

Practical wisdom involves the intellectual grasp of the activity of the will considered in itself as an object. This involves the activity of self-restraint as an object of willing. One sense in which the act of the will can be considered in itself is that according to which the act of willing is itself a good, and this, as opposed to its opposite, non willing (*non velle*). Doing something is better than doing nothing. But it is rare that one ever encounters these as two options for choice. This internal reflexive act is always part of a more extended, complex act of willing.

An example may help us here. I may encounter a situation in which I am called upon to tell the truth to a friend. This act of honesty may involve painful revelations to someone I care for. In terms of the act of choice before me, I have the option to speak the truth or to lie. Thus I might hesitate before I speak. But in addition, I have the capacity to dis-engage myself from the choice before me. This disengagement involves the choice between willing to choose (*velle*) or refraining from choice (*non velle*). I have chosen to call this a disengagement, because it involves not so much a rejection of the choice, but a positive act of self-restraint on the part of the will. This act is rational and involves the dynamic between the two affections in the will. It is the same sort of movement I encounter whenever I exert control over my actions or my inclinations to act. I know that telling the truth to my friend is important: not to do so could undermine our relationship. However, I may be reticent to give my friend this information. I may be afraid of her reaction; I may feel it is not appropriate information for her to have, the information may be confidential. Accordingly, when asked, I would deliberate and produce a dictate of right reason relative to this situation. In the presence of this dictate, I might choose to refrain from choice. In other words, in the presence of my friend, I might judge that telling the truth is the best course of action, and yet not do so. I would not lie to her, I would simply remain silent. This act of self-restraint would safeguard both the free-dom and the rationality of the will, since I do not choose entirely counter to the conclusion "tell her the truth." I don't have to lie in order not to tell the truth. Scotus states that moral choice does not follow; that is, there is no moral habit of truthfulness generated in the will, which would only imply that my will need not respond to my intellect's judgment. What is important about the moral implications of this act lies in the extent to which the affection for justice truly governs the choice to act or not. If fear prevents me from engaging myself in speaking the truth, then the affection for possession (or my own good) has taken the upper hand.

In order to illustrate the importance of the reflexive act for moral character, consider another aspect of this truth-telling situation. Had I previously chosen to live my life according to the truth, to attempt to will rightly every time the opportunity presented itself, to integrate my life around truth in moral living, then this request for truth would not be an isolated incident for choice. My overriding concern for integrity of life would inform my deliberation. I might be aware of fear over my friend's reaction to the truth, but this fear would also lie within my control. I would acknowledge its presence, but not allow it to determine my choice.

The reflexive moral choice involved here is the choice for a moral orientation of life, and not just individual moral choices as they present themselves. It is a moment when the will looks at itself as in a mirror and asks the question, "what sort of direction do I wish to give myself in the choices I make?" This question does not come at the beginning of the moral life, but rather as the result of many years of life experience. Some people may never face this choice consciously. It represents a fundamental moral option, but not one which occurs prior to moral living. It is the result of moral living and intensifies the act of moral deliberation and choice. It is a commitment to moral action which joins natural inclination to freedom.

When the object of such a choice is the will's very own act, then one is able to will "right willing" for itself, as a good in itself. In this case, the same conditions apply as for an external object, that is, the intellect apprehends this object "according to the rules from which *praxis* can be caused."[29] These rules certainly involve the basic, first principle of *praxis* "Do good, avoid evil." Scotus's version of this principle, "*Deus diligendus est*" (God is to be loved) belongs also to these "rules," as would the commands of the Decalogue. As these rules apply to the internal act of choice, they could be summarized under the command "choose rightly," that is, choose to choose rightly in every moral act. Here is revealed the self-determination of the moral will which chooses right action for itself alone, as a *per se* good, and not because of any consideration of reward or future good.[30]

---

[29]   *Lectura* Prologue in *Will and Morality*, p. 137.

[30]   This is not to say that the only *per se* good to be discovered by the will is internal to

The movement of the will relative to itself and according to the first principle of *praxis* begins a process of moral self-perfection. With the help of the virtue of prudence, the will chooses to choose rightly. The focus on moral choosing as the functioning of the moral will moves the discussion from a means-end paradigm (which one finds with Albert and Thomas) to one in which the activity itself is the "goal in becoming": a present, not a future good. Like Aristotle's musician, the moral agent concentrates on this act, on this performance, and seeks to make it as perfect as possible.[31]

Thus, the importance of prudence is two-fold. First, it defines the will's act as rational: it presents options, involves deliberation, and gives counsel on a level of external-choice. In addition, prudence defines the rational act of the will insofar as it considers the choice as an object of right willing in light of proper moral motivation. This involves the will's self-conscious moral orientation. To will rightly right willing is to discover the coincidence of activity and end, the agreement of *praxis* with its object. In this case, there are no rules external to the act itself: the act of right willing provides its own rule. Here, priority and agreement do not constitute a vicious circle, but actually refer to the same act seen first, from the perspective of intellection and second, from that of volition. Thus, moral wisdom for Scotus, as for Aquinas, involves the cooperation of reasoning and desire. However, for Scotus, this cooperation is defined entirely within the realm of *praxis* and does not appeal to any natural tendency on the part of the will as appetite for the universal good.

Scotus's focus on the ability to refrain from choice (*non velle*) enables him to explain more easily how even very good people still err. It is easy to understand the moral expert or virtuous person who, though not vicious, is not always virtuous. They are not virtuous because they do

---

its own activity. Such a discovery can also occur in the case of an object external to the will. For example, metaphysical reflection upon the essential order within reality enables prudence to discover *ens infinitum* which is also *bonum infinitum* at the summit of reality. This discovery informs the prudential awareness of the principle *Deus diligendus est.* See Wolter's "Native Freedom of the Will", 151. This discovery, however, would be the result of speculation rather than an immediate reflection upon *praxis,* therefore it would belong to moral science and support the continuing prudential assessment. The internal act of self-reflection is, by contrast, contingent, more immediate and requires only self-reflection. It is a better starting point for a practical science.

[31] *Nicomachean Ethics* I, 7, 1098a 10-15.

not act as they should; they choose not to act at all. No amount of truthful behavior in my past determines how I will act toward my friend. Certainly, refraining from a moral choice is a serious matter, especially for the moral expert. But such unwillingness to act would not run as radically counter to character and past experience as would the outright rejection of the morally good option, that is, if I lied rather than tell the truth. My moral character, once developed, does not necessitate moral choices, but neither is it arbitrary.

Conclusions

Moral character develops through concrete experience, reflection and judgment, followed by right action. The will reveals its rationality in its relationship both to external objects and to its own acts. The self-conscious moral choice on the part of the will involves a moral orientation which informs, but does not determine, all subsequent choices. The will can choose to choose rightly, and thus at a fundamental level choose an activity which realizes the moral end in an immediate manner. This self-directed movement toward moral perfection is aided by the presence of prudence as practical wisdom.

In his analysis of the influence of virtue, Scotus does not reject the importance of natural inclinations within the morally good act. In I,17, he defends the manner in which his understanding of partial co-causality provides a better explanation, for it protects the value of natural virtue and presents it in light of the perfection of the morally good act, which is essentially an act of love. This causal perspective enables the Franciscan to analyze moral goodness in such a way as to reconcile both freedom and natural inclination by means of efficient causality.

The use of an efficient co-causal discussion also permits a nuanced definition of virtue. Scotus's treatment of virtue involves both inclination and excellent moral action. The natural, habitual dimension of activity has a potential moral significance. It is *mere* practical habit. The moral or superior dimension of the inclination stems from the activity of right reasoning or prudence. Clearly, virtue is moral virtue solely by means of the operation of right reasoning and the conformity of the inclination to its dictates.

The potentially moral inclination toward generosity becomes actually moral when the dictates of right reasoning judge the generous act to be appropriate. It is not appropriate for a person with a family to give all the family's money away, nor is it morally praiseworthy to spend one's time working at a soup kitchen, when one's own children are in need of parental time and attention. The appropriate expression of the inclination toward generosity is subordinate to the reflection and judgment of right reasoning. This means, of course, that what constitutes moral generosity for one may not be identical to the moral generosity of another. Each person must determine the appropriate expression of the virtuous inclination.

The distinction between habitual inclination and moral virtue enhances an understanding of the place of virtue within moral activity according to Scotus. In the strictest sense, virtue is not an essential part of the moral realm, since it operates naturally. However, since natural inclination toward the good is indeed a fundamental aspect of the will, the free choice which constitutes moral action relies heavily upon the natural dimension and upon the presence of natural factors contributing to and facilitating moral goodness. Consequently, although important for the moral life, virtue is not a central, organizing factor in Scotist theory. Right reasoning emerges as key element within the morally righteous agent and the morally good life.

Moral perfection, then, requires a dynamic for loving which is both natural and free, and involves the self-perfecting operation of the will. The natural inclination of the will toward the good, and that mutuality of will and intellect in the affection for justice create a process by which moral excellence, that excellence of the will in conformity with right reasoning, is attained. Virtues intensify the moral dynamic and enable the individual to make judgments and perform right actions quickly. They enhance moral actions by enhancing the ability of the moral person to move from judgment to action.

The Franciscan's distinction between the natural and moral dimensions is at the heart of this distinction between virtue as inclination and the moral life as free. The natural is necessary, and no rewards are to be given for that over which we have no control. Just as no one is to be rewarded for the habitually generous act, neither is one to be praised for the act stemming from a type of "moral luck." The rich person who can be generous because of family wealth, and not because of any personal responsibility, deserves no special praise. Virtue for Scotus is more to be identified with motivation than with performance: moral excellence is the perfection of motivation.

The description of virtue and its relationship to the morally good act brings us to a final aspect: the role and importance of the rational will. Moral choice lies beyond the realm of natural virtue which is one circumstance among many whose conformity is determined by right reasoning. Virtue is not the subject of deliberation or choice. The moral dimension is solely the function of the will's freedom in accordance with right reason. Moral excellence does not depend upon specific virtues, but upon the exercise of a rational will. The virtues may be natural conditions for the good act, but they are not central elements for a theory of human excellence.

Scotus's presentation of virtue is clearly more Anselmian-Augustinian than Aristotelian, and yet there are aspects which do not conflict with passages in the *Nicomachean Ethics*. The significant aspect of Scotist thought, clearly, is the centrality of the will as moral component and the importance of freedom for moral goodness. Nowhere in Aristotle does freedom take on such an important role. The necessity for virtue, according to Scotus, is found within the will where it partially constitutes but is never totally responsible for moral goodness. The natural dimension, since it is necessary, can never belong to the dimension of deliberation and choice. Virtues appear in this context as dispositions or practical habits based upon natural inclinations toward the good. They surround the will as pieces surround the center of the wind chime.

In response to the 12th century discussion of moral *habitus*, Scotus emphasizes the moral realm as that of dynamic *praxis* proper to deliberation and choice. In this more narrow context virtue is linked to activity within the will which relates directly to moral decisions. Broader natural inclinations toward rational action are identified with natural causality. Scotus's discussion focuses on the activities proper to decision-making. Virtue enhances the ability to make a moral choice in a timely manner.

In response to the 13th century discussion of moral and theological virtues, Scotus integrates the two as natural causes into a special order of causality. There they intensify the activity of the will in making moral choices. The decision to consider both moral and theological virtues as belonging to the same causal order indicates the anthropocentric perspective Scotus has chosen. The moral life is not a separate order from the life of grace. The virtues together form a continuum which stretches from human to divine reality and joins all life in growth toward holiness. It is freedom which distinguishes moral choice as moral. The virtues intensify and integrate the formation of character, but they do not constitute moral goodness in the absence of moral reasoning or choice.

There is no sense in which the moral goal ever involves the kind of perfection of action which is either free from error or automatic. The key aspect of moral virtue is that it is virtue freely chosen, and under the direction of right reasoning. Repetitive actions or learned behavior do not, of themselves, constitute moral character. The element of free and rational choice governs the moral realm and insofar as virtues participate in this realm, they contribute to moral character.

five

ℳoral Reasoning
and
Discernment:
Prudence

To this point, the discussion has focused on moral goodness as it appears in actions and on virtues as they influence decisions. The present chapter intensifies this reflection with a focus on the person in the activity of moral decision-making. Prudence is a key virtue for moral living because it works most closely with the will and perfects the process of deliberation and choice. For Scotus, this means that, if loving rightly constitutes moral excellence, then the goal of all *praxis* (practical living) is the development of a will capable of appropriate response to the goods surrounding it. For us, this means that each person can be understood according to the analogy of the wind chime. It is not just action, but our very selves which are meant to be beautiful and harmonious. As practical wisdom, prudence perfects the natural qualities which make this beauty possible.

As we saw in the preceding chapter, prudence governs the domain of moral choice in two ways. First, it offers guidance in moments of deliberation regarding objects and options external to the will: e.g., whether or not to tell the truth. Second, it guides the reflexive activity of rational freedom in choosing a moral orientation: e.g., living a life in the light of truth. These two dimensions of moral living reveal the close relationship between moral choice and moral character. My moral choices both reveal and constitute my character. My moral living reveals both the beauty of action and the beauty of character. Integrity involves both external behavior and internal moral motivation. The goal of *praxis* is immanent to the moral person: it creates character. In medieval iconography, prudence appears as a woman with two faces: one looking forward and the other looking in a mirror.[1] Scotus integrates these two "faces" into the activity of rational freedom, as the moral person is both aware of circumstances around her and of her own moral orientation.

In the study of ethical theory today, we often distinguish the character or virtue-based tradition from the theoretical or principle-based. While such a distinction has obvious advantages for a philosophy curriculum, it has the immense disadvantage of fragmenting the domain of moral reasoning in such a way that the orders of virtue and principle seem to be at odds with one another. The discussion of moral decision-making appears to involve a choice between the primacy of principle (as abstract reasoning of a highly theoretical nature, to which no exceptions are allowable) and that of virtue (learned dispositions toward good actions taken from experience, and derived from the culture in which one finds oneself). The impression given, a bit unfairly perhaps, is that of two extremes: either moral living involves absolute principles which always obtain, or is simply relative to culture. In Alasdaire MacIntyre's insightful study, *After Virtue*,[2] this fragmentation reveals itself in the so-called choice between Aristotelian and Kantian traditions. More recently, Daniel Mark Nelson, in *The Priority of Prudence*,[3] deals with the issues of virtue and natural law in Aquinas according to this very opposition. Nelson argues that prudence for Aquinas belongs more to the virtue-paradigm than to the principle-paradigm.

A solution to the contemporary moral malaise so well described by MacIntyre may not be in the victory of one moral model over another, but in the effective integration of both *virtue* and *principle* into a coherent moral perspective. This integration should take place at the level of moral reasoning, where issues of virtue and principle have their source. In this chapter we examine, first, how Scotus presents moral reasoning in the virtue of prudence. In light of his presentation, we reflect upon the way in which prudence unifies the moral domain (both virtue and principle) around the activity of moral reasoning and decision making.

[1]   See Robert J. Mulvaney, "Wisdom, Time and Avarice in St. Thomas Aquinas's Treatment on Prudence" in *The Modern Schoolman* 69, March/May 1992, p. 450.
[2]   Notre Dame, 1981, 1986.
[3]   Penn State Press 1992.

The Presentation of Prudence

In Book VI of the *Nicomachean Ethics* Aristotle defines prudence (*phronesis*) as the intellectual virtue proper to moral excellence. "Necessarily, then, practical wisdom is a truthful rational characteristic of acting in matters involving what is good for us."[4] Prudence is that virtue essential to moral deliberation, decision-making, choice and ultimately to the experience of the human moral excellence of *eudaimonia*. Christian medieval responses to Aristotle's moral theory varied, as philosophers and theologians worked to harmonize the Greek moral vision (with its heavy emphasis upon learned, habitual excellence) with the experience of Christian revelation and the human realities of sin/error, grace, forgiveness and the possibility of conversion.

An important tradition for the Latin understanding of prudence was Stoicism.[5] Stoic thinkers tended to collapse the distinction between the areas of theoretical and practical reasoning, identifying prudence (*prudentia*) with wisdom (*sapientia*). The wise person was prudent, having a grasp of the eternal order (eternal law) and transcending the realm of contingent experience. In the 12th century, most of the discussion of prudence took the text of Cicero's *Rhetoric*: "Prudence is of things good and evil, and the science (*scientia*) of each" (II,53).[6] Early 13th century thinkers such as William of Auxerre and Philip the Chancellor identified two different types of prudence: prudence-science and prudence-virtue. The distinction involved the clarity of knowledge at each level. Prudence-science attains knowledge (*scire*) of principles and enjoys a high level of certainty: the certainty of science. Prudence-virtue is not called knowledge, but rather acquaintance (*cognoscere*): it involves an awareness of particulars. In this, the early 13th century reflection upon Aristotle emphasized the scientific quality of ethics, rather than its practical aspect. Scotus's emphasis on the importance of the contingent particular draws his reflection in the direction of ethics as *practical* science.

In Scotus's writings we discover both virtue/character concerns along with the importance of principle as key dimensions of moral living. Moral decisions involve right appetite and right reasoning, thus

---

[4] At 1140b 20-23, slightly modified Ostwald translation.

[5] See Gérard Verbeke, *The Presence of Stoicism in Medieval Thought*, Washington: Catholic University Press 1983.

[6] Pierre Aubenque, "La <Phronésis> chez les Stoiciens" in *La Prudence chez Aristote*, Paris: PUF 1986₃, pp.184-5.

both learned behavior and reflected insight. The moral community is essential both for appetitive and rational development in the moral agent. For Scotus, moral choices and the exercise of prudence are neither purely theoretical exercises of abstract reasoning, nor are they the immediate result of a "gut feeling" about what course of action to take. Rather, they are the harmonious blend of both.

In earlier chapters we discussed the double constitution of the will: the affection for justice and the affection for possession. In the same manner, we see that prudence has a double dimension. Scotus follows Philip the Chancellor in distinguishing the first as "moral science." This involves intellectual knowledge of the first practical principle ("God is to be loved") as well as any moral norms which might flow logically from this. These would be norms promoting love for God. The second dimension is referred to as prudence itself. This emerges in the operation of rational reflection and choice. The prudential dynamic is generated from acts of choice: from the interaction of the two affections in light of principle. Prudence is not abstract reasoning, but an habitual activity immediate to practical decision-making.

> I say the definition of prudence ought to be understood as active, proximate habit, acquired from acts. Just as arts are the habit of the expert, so are actions to prudence, since the habits of arts and morals are quasi remote to direction, because they are universal; but prudence, generated by actions, is particular and near to direction. This is necessary, otherwise no practical science [would exist] which deals with art or *praxis*.[7]

In other words, prudence is not a characteristic like strength. The bodybuilder, for instance, is strong even when not lifting weights. The prudent person is more like the dancer: identified within the performance of the activity. I am really only a dancer when I dance, yet I can let the grace of the dance inform the way I walk, the way I stand, the way I move. The prudent person relies upon learned behavior and training: the virtue itself is generated by actions. Such a person continually acts out of an attitude of self-controlled rationality. Thus, to say that prudence is tied closely to concrete acts of decision and choice is not to fragment moral living into specific instances of moral decision-making. Rather, it is to identify the dynamic aspect of moral rationality which

---

[7]   *Ordinatio* Prologue, n. 351 (1:228).

underpins human living, just as graceful movements identify the dancer.

When we see this in terms of the two affections within the will, the situation plays itself out in the following manner. Let us return to my decision-process of chapters two and three. I have some time this afternoon and face options such as working in the garden, doing some reading, writing this chapter. In facing this decision, I am aware of the two affections which draw me to certain options. The affection for possession looks for those aspects of this decision which benefit me personally. The affection for justice turns my attention to impersonal concerns present in this decision: values and consequences which lie beyond my own benefit. The judgment, whatever it might be, belongs to prudence and directs my actions in an immediate manner. In making the judgment, prudence draws upon the deliberation over options but is immediate to the action I am about to perform. Proper judgment and execution reinforce and strengthen the activity of prudence within me.

Now imagine a choice in which one of the options involves moral error or sin. In working on this chapter, I see the possibility of plagiarizing work done by another. Here enters the domain of moral principle in a more theoretical manner. In other words, not only do I consider the practical aspects of this concrete situation, but I also bring to my consideration theoretical principles which would belong to any moral life. For example, had I previously committed my life to truth as a moral orientation, then the value of truth and its integration into my life would provide an overlay for this decision process. The importance of consistency with my own life commitment, or coherence with principles I value would influence how I view certain options.

Scotus presents several dimensions to moral rationality. In these we see that, as an intellectual virtue, prudence participates in the cognitional activities of abstraction and intuition. Moral reasoning has access to the higher domains of principle, to the generalized level of learned moral knowledge, to the immediate elements within the concrete moral decision and, finally, to the data of revelation. The judgment of prudence seeks to bring together all these levels of rational reflection into a decision about what ought to be done.

For ethics to be a practical science, it must have a dimension which is validly scientific. Here, mathematics serves Scotus's reflection well. He compares the highest domain of moral reasoning with geometry, for some conclusions are deduced from first principles of *praxis.* For example, there are some goods which reveal themselves in light of reflection upon the nature of rational beings. As we saw in chapter three, proper reflection upon human nature as rational and upon the activity of understanding reveals that falsehood is not an appropriate object for the intellect.

> Every judgment begins with something certain. Now the first judg-ment about the appropriateness cannot pre-suppose some knowl-edge determined by another intellect; otherwise it would not be first. Hence it presupposes something certain but judged by this intellect, namely: the nature of the agent and the power by which he acts together with the essential notion of the act. If these three notions are given, no other knowledge is needed to judge whether or not this particular act is suited to this agent and this faculty.... Knowing what it means to attain knowledge, it would also be clear to him what it is not appropriate for his mind to reach.[8]

From the affirmation that falsehood is inappropriate for human intel-lection, Scotus concludes that lying is never morally admissible. This conclusion belongs to a category of moral truths derived from reflec-tion upon human nature: a more theoretical body of moral knowledge. It can, of course, be verified by concrete experience of the negative consequences of lying. However, as we know, lying does not always have immediate negative consequences.

In addition to such theoretical moral truths, moral reasoning has access to generalized information gained through experience. For this, experience and training within a community are essential. When speaking of justice, for example, Scotus claims that a precise calculation is impossible and that there is a great latitude in the mean. In this he rejects the position of Richard of Middleton who argued that there is a high degree of precision in questions of justice. In contrast, Scotus explains that commutative justice can fall within a number of degrees between the extremes.

> Indeed there is great latitude in this mean that commutative jus-tice regards or looks to, and within this latitude one does not attain an indivisible point of equivalence between one thing and anoth-er, because so far as this is concerned, it is impossible as it were to

---

[8]   Quodlibet Question 18 in *God and Creatures* 18.13, pp. 402-3.

bring about an exchange [that is precisely equivalent] and it becomes just in any degree between these extremes. But what this latitude is and to what it extends is known sometimes through positive law, and at other times through custom.[9]

The theoretical and learned dimensions of moral reasoning point to an obvious insight: it is one thing to know that lying is wrong, it is another to know when and where truth telling is appropriate. The example raised earlier about a friend's request for information reveals this distinction very well. If we add that the information requested was confidential, then we see that the option of silence or self-restraint is the morally appropriate course of action. In this case, I neither lie nor do I reveal what was given me in confidence. It is not appropriate to lie, nor is it imperative to tell the truth. The judgment that silence is the best course of action requires attention to the demands of moral science ("never lie") and to the demands of the concrete situation in which I find myself. The activity of prudence, the excellence of moral reasoning, reveals the dynamic and harmonious blend of theory and training as I seek to promote goodness in an imperfect world.

Both these levels belong to prudence by virtue of the intellectual act of abstraction. In abstraction, the intellect reasons in a mediated manner, either by syllogism (in the case of the highest level of principle) or by generalization from concrete instances (in the case of moral knowledge which is learned through experience). Both of these can be called "moral science." Because it is an intellectual virtue, prudence participates in moral science in the form of fundamental moral insights and the first principle of *praxis,* "Do good and avoid evil." Such scientific knowledge is the result of abstractive intellection and reaches a stage of generalization which is independent of particulars. Moral science both derives from mediated reasoning and requires a process of mediated reasoning in order to inform moral conclusions.

The truths proper to the highest level of moral science are necessary and universal, originating in a deductive process which is not directly related to action. In III, 36, Scotus states that moral science is a type of "special moral knowledge" in the absence of experience and remote

---

[9]   IV, 15, 2, art. 2 (n.15) in *Political and Economic Philosophy,* p. 55.

from acts of concrete choice.[10] There can be, Scotus states, necessary
truths about contingent affairs, for example, about the fact that a stone
will fall when dropped, even though the fall of the stone is itself a contingent state of affairs. There can be scientific knowledge about contingent affairs, yet this is not the same as deliberative knowledge about the
same state of affairs. "Hence even though something contingent be the
object of a deliberative habit, such as prudence, as regards those conclusions one can necessarily draw about such a contingent thing, that same
item is the object of a scientific habit."[11] Thus, while moral science is
accessible to prudence as right reasoning, it is imperfect, incomplete
and remote from the act of moral judgment. Without specific information and concrete data gained from the particular, no moral decision
can be reached. It is not enough for me to know that lying is wrong; I
must also learn when and where to tell the truth.

In addition to the domain of moral science, Scotus speaks of prudence as an immediate cognitional act. His discussion of the immediacy
of prudential judgment resembles his presentation of the second act of
intellection: intuition. The originality of Scotus's discussion of prudence may indeed lie in his discussion of intuition. The activity of prudence as the expression of practical rational excellence involves both
rational, cognitional acts: abstraction and intuition. In an intuitive act,
moral reasoning operates at a level immediate to experience and with
no intervention by the mental *image.* "Perfect intuition is the awareness
of a present existential situation...."[12] It is this Scotist epistemology
involving a two-fold cognitional act which determines the operation of
prudence as right reasoning in the context of concrete moral situations.

Both in his description of intuitive acts and prudential judgment,
Scotus specifies the *immediacy* of the act as the decisive factor. In his
Subtle Questions on the Metaphysics, he describes intuition as follows:

> ... *our* intellects have a kind of intellectual cognition whereby we
> know immediately a singular existent, even though we do not

[10]   *Will and Morality,* p. 401. Scotus also calls moral science "remote from direction" in
     the *Ordinatio* Prologue, in order to contrast it with prudence as "active and proxi-
     mate". See n. 351 (1:228)

[11]   *Lectura* Prologue in *Will and Morality,* p. 141.

[12]   Wolter, "Duns Scotus on Intuition, Memory and Our Knowledge of Individuals"
     in *Philosophical Theology...,* p. 101.

know its singularity (or that by which it is singularized); this mode of cognition is called *visio* or *intuitive cognition.*[13]

Prudence is discussed in a similar manner:

> Hence prudence is simply a habit that is more immediately direct-
> ed towards practice, so that a prudent person knows immediately
> the means to use and does not have to reason backwards from prin-
> ciples to other prior principles. A science, like moral philosophy,
> however, is only mediately practical, because it teaches how one
> should behave in regard to actions through a process of reason-
> ing.[14]

In this passage, prudence is contrasted with moral science, the result of an abstract and theoretical cognitional act. Since the intellect is capable of both acts, and since (as both Day[15] and Wolter[16] maintain) intuition may include all that abstraction does (plus the certainty which comes from immediacy), then prudence (as an intellectual virtue) participates fully in both cognitional acts. It thus has access to abstract moral princi- ple and, more importantly, to concrete moral data.

If we return to the truth-telling situation, we understand more clearly how the judgment of prudence participates in but differs signifi- cantly from moral science. My normal truthful behavior is based both on learned experience about the results of lying, but also upon a consid- eration of the value of truth and the inconsistency of a life based upon deception. So I carry about in my "moral science" category conclusions such as "lying is wrong." But, along with this fundamental moral truth, I might also have insights gained from experiences. These might include "telling the truth to friends is a good" or "always tell the truth gently when it is going to hurt." All such conclusions, theoretical and general- ized, inform the deliberation and judgment of what to do right now in

---

[13]   Book VII, q. 15 (Vivès 7:438b).

[14]   *Will and Morality*, pp. 141-143.

[15]   See Sebastian Day, *Intuitive Cognition: A Key to the Significance of Later Scholastics*, Franciscan Institute Publications 1947.

[16]   "Intuitive cognition, on the other hand, while it may include all the data or infor- mation found in a corresponding abstractive cognition, invariably includes some- thing more, viz., that additional knowledge or information of the fact that it exists." "The Formal Distinction" in *John Duns Scotus 1265-1965*, Ryan/Bonansea, CUA Press 1965, p. 58. Reprinted in *Philosophical Theology...*, p. 39.

the case of my friend. But I must also bring to bear the nature of the truth which is to be told, the nature of the harm, the appropriateness of the present moment, the state of mind of my friend, and my ability to be tactful at this time. All of these more precise bits of information are critical to the judgment of prudence and they do not belong to moral science. It may be the appropriate course of action to disengage from this choice: neither lie nor tell the truth.

Scotus does not present a moral theory which directly addresses the existence of a "moral intuition" or immediate grasp of goodness. Despite this, he certainly provides for such a position. By means of the act of intuition, the moral agent has direct access to the concrete situation and thus to significant moral data to be used in the decision-making process. This is an important point of contrast with Aquinas who defended a position which involved mediated cognitive access to reality. And, in contrast to Bonaventure, Scotus unifies theoretical and practical reasoning processes in the virtue of prudence, whose judgment never causally determines the act of the will.

As we have seen, for ethics to be a practical science it requires both a scientific and a practical dimension. The scientific and practical dynamic within the prudential will is developed over time. The integration of principle and virtue occurs through concrete acts of moral choice. Prudence is an acquired intellectual virtue, whose natural excellence involves both rational norms and particular circumstances. Like the artist, the moral agent seeks to create beauty, balancing responses with concrete situations, under the guidance of general principles.

Prudence is that virtue which is naturally generated by the rational will within its operation of loving. The natural appetite for moral rectitude enters into dynamic interaction with the desire for the good. Increased interaction of the two affections focuses and develops the natural ability to reason and choose rightly. Thus prudence is the acquired habit of rational, moral excellence. It is the direct result of the will's capacity for rational loving, its fundamental love for goodness, and the objective order in nature constituted by divine love.

Love for God is not the only piece of rational information at hand for moral actions. There is found within revelation a more precise set of norms by which the first principle of *praxis* is to be actualized. Found in the last seven commands of the Decalogue, these norms deal with love for others. If we truly seek the moral goal of love for God, then we must follow the command to love one another. The rational will has access to moral information and develops the excellence of self-control through the virtue of prudence. As moral science, prudence determines right action based upon an understanding of means leading to a designated end (love for God); as practical virtue it directs this action toward a morally good end.

The Decalogue plays a prominent role in Scotus's understanding of moral goodness. For any moral agents who have serious doubts about the rationality of a decision, the precepts of the Decalogue provide a touchstone against which it can be measured. God's desire for our behavior is significant moral information for any choice. In addition, the moral appetite never functions alone, just as abstract reflection is never sufficient for moral judgment, nor does intuition function as sole arbiter of moral goodness. Reasoning (which involves acts of intuition and abstraction) and appetite are meant to be *consona* or in harmony, and a certain primacy is given to principle, even with the possibility of exceptional cases.

Finally, Scotus appears to assume the existence of a moral community in which dialogue and consultation inform every human decision. His is not a presentation where appetite is suspect or where it is seen as non-rational. Rather, appetite is human and, therefore, rational: participating in both a desire for justice and for self-preservation.

Moral rationality extends beyond mere abstract discussion of principle. The moral ability to reason correctly is not simply determined by the number and variety of past experiences. There lies within each moral choice certain individual elements which are beyond the determination of principles or past behavior. These elements influence the direction of moral reflection and, to some extent, the final decision in a way which principle cannot predict. Objective moral direction is provided by revelation, thus providing Scotus with a dependable standard for moral action: God's command of love. The prohibitions of the Decalogue represent the basic values of moral living. I cannot act against these without harming my moral life. There is, then, a degree to which I can predict my future moral choices: actions I will never choose under any circumstances. In addition, there is a dimension which I must leave open. I can predict with certainty that I will always seek to act rationally. I cannot predict what those rational actions will be.

The Activity of Moral Reasoning

Scotus presents prudence as more than just a virtue: it is a dynamic activity of rationality within the concrete dimension of human living. Prudence is not an inclination like strength or skill. These can be attributed to a person even when they are not in use. Prudence is that sort of quality which must be active to be possessed. It is the manifestation of the affection for justice which governs human living. It is living out the demands of a life of self-control. This dynamic discussion of prudence points to the artistic imagery which is present in Scotus's discussion of moral living and the operation of moral rationality.

In *Ordinatio* I, 17 Scotus describes moral goodness as harmony inherent in an act. Like beauty, goodness is the proper integration of all conditions necessary for an act to be *whole*. The judgment of such wholeness in a good act is compared to an artistic assessment, immediately grasped by the expert. Scotus differentiates the prudent person from one who "knows the science of morals" through an analogy taken from art. One may have theoretical artistic knowledge and not understand the craft as well as another who has developed her talent "simply from experience."

An analogy from music may clarify this point. There might be a person who has studied musical theory (notation, composition, etc.) but has never learned to play an instrument. This person can speak with some authority on the proper performance technique for a given piece of music, despite the fact that she cannot herself perform the piece. A second person may have enormous native musical talent; she has taught herself to play the piano, but unfortunately, cannot read music easily. She can reproduce music with a high degree of accuracy, but cannot explain the theory behind her performance. A third person has both native talent, learned ability and has been trained in music theory. This third person could compose an original piece of music and explain why she has chosen this form, this notation, these dynamics. She has both the theoretical and the practical knowledge necessary to be creative and original. She knows what can be performed and what should be performed. The other two might be able to compose an original piece, but the first would not have the depth of knowledge (lacking experience) and the second would not be able to explain why she has chosen to compose the piece in the precise manner she has. In addition, the actual composition would be more difficult for them; it might be impossible if the music had a high degree of complexity. The self-taught musician would have to compensate for her lack of theory with an extremely good memory.

Similarly, there might be a person with a high degree of abstract moral knowledge, but with little or no lived moral experience. Another might have a good body of experiential moral knowledge, but little theoretical moral education. A third may have both learned knowledge and lived experience. In the case of an unexpected moral decision, it is clear that the third person would possess the moral resources for the best decision, even though the others might still choose rightly. The third person would have the ability to be creative with the case at hand; she would be aware of more options to consider, aware of the basis for moral principle, aware of which aspects of the situation to consider more seriously. Scotus's discussion of moral rationality integrates the spectrum of moral reflection to include the highest levels of principle with the most attentive concern for specific details. This sort of integration, like musical expertise, requires a lifetime of training. Moral "attentiveness" is not just operative in moments of crisis, but is the manifestation of rational attention which is always expressed in the life of the formed moral person. Prudence, then, does not just appear in moments of deliberation and decision, it is the guiding principle of rationality within human living.

When we understand this artistic dimension in light of the act of intuition, we find some very interesting implications for moral decision-making. The concrete moral context for any decision contains specific information for the moral subject. Moral affections register an objective reality or whole which is not mediated by a mental image, but is the result of a direct cognition. Scotus suggests that intuitive cognition has access to whatever sense perception does, albeit in an indistinct manner.[17] While in Aquinas my moral feelings provide me with information about myself and are thus an indirect source for moral data, for Scotus my moral feelings tell me something about external reality, and are thus a foundational piece of data for a moral decision. One might argue, then, that Scotus actually provides a more *objective* basis (that is, external to the subject) for moral judgment than does his Dominican predecessor. There is an objective wholeness about the morally good act, a wholeness which Scotus believes can be grasped by any rational agent.

---

[17]   See *Questions on the Metaphysics,* II, q. 3, nn. 23-25. Wolter discusses this text in "Duns Scotus on Intuition," pp. 109-110.

An interesting example of the activity of prudential judgment can be found in Jane Austen's novel, *Pride and Prejudice*. In this encounter between the willful Elizabeth Bennet and the proud Fitzwilliam Darcy, there is a moment when the revelation of truth becomes extremely important. George Wickham, a young military officer, has spread rumors which accuse Darcy of dishonorable behavior. The rumors cause everyone to consider Darcy something of a scoundrel. Elizabeth raises the subject with Darcy on two occasions, and in both he refuses to speak of the matter. Finally, after she rejects his proposal of marriage and accuses him of inhumane behavior relative to Wickham, Darcy writes Elizabeth and tells her the truth about Wickham.

In this simple example, we see the levels of rational reflection referred to earlier, as well as the demands of a present moment which require a change of behavior. Darcy is a man of honor; he knows the importance of truth and integrity. In addition, he grew up with George Wickham; he has learned experience of the man's character and knows he cannot be trusted. Prior to his decision to reveal the truth to Elizabeth, there are also circumstances which might justify truth-telling out of self-defense. Wickham is ruining his character, his public reputation, with lies. He might be justified in acting out of his healthy self-interest (affection for possession) and "save his own name." However, he does not choose to do so. When asked, he remains silent, choosing not to speak of Wickham at all. As the reader discovers later, he has acted not only out of a sense of personal integrity, but also to save the reputation of Georgianna, his sister. The revelation of truth would require information which would have harmed his sister's name. Thus, in light of all these levels of information and circumstance, Darcy chooses not to disclose information about Wickham's character. He chooses what appears to be the most honorable action. This choice affects the way Elizabeth views him, and ultimately influences her refusal of his marriage proposal.

He does, however, change his mind. The day following her refusal, Darcy writes to Elizabeth to tell her the truth about himself. He does so not to further his own prospects with her, but rather because of the requirements of his character. Justice demands that she allow him the opportunity to clear his own name, at least with her. In revealing the painful events surrounding Georgianna, he asks Elizabeth to hold the information confidential. While Darcy does not explain what has brought about this change of behavior, he does say that his choice to remain silent was due to his inability to ascertain and control how much truth he should reveal.[18] The letter offers him the opportunity to weigh carefully what he reveals.

In this example we see the dimensions of moral rationality simultaneously at work. The concerns belong to levels of character and integrity, experience, foresight and the constraints of the present moment. Darcy's actions reveal the importance of timing and finding the appropriate manner for action. Both in his silence and in writing the letter, Darcy acts according to his sense of honor. Both actions are informed by his concern for integrity. Both reveal his character as it responds to the unfolding course of events. At one moment it is appropriate to keep silence; at another it is important to speak the truth. In neither action does he seek to further his own good at the expense of others.

Darcy's change of mind about what to do in this situation reveals also the importance of freedom as self-control. Prior to the letter, the freedom he exhibits is that of self-restraint. He chooses neither to lie nor to tell the truth. The following day, however, he concludes that the truth in this instance should be told, yet told discretely. Thus, his moral reflection is entirely within the domain of his own self-control. The discussion of the influence of virtue in right choice is also significant here. In chapter four, we saw that the prudent person is described as one who "acts swiftly" and is able to reason "immediately" to what should be done. In this context, Darcy's reflection does not end when he reaches the first decision. He continues to reflect, based upon new information and upon the constraints of the situation as they reveal themselves. Because he is attentive to the moral dimensions of this situation, he quickly revises his conclusions in light of new developments: i.e., the extent to which Elizabeth and her family are blind to Wickham's real character.

Moral education for Scotus entails the gradual integration of all inclinations (natural and virtuous) under the *aegis* of the will. This means that in the morally mature person, a high degree of integration has occurred. This person would have natural inclinations, as we saw in chapter four, but they would all be within the will's control and potentially useful for moral deliberation and action. Because they fall within the control of rational freedom, they would not interfere with the exercise of moral action. For instance, in the example where I fear telling my

[18] Darcy writes: "You may possibly wonder why all this was not told you last night. But I was not then master enough of myself to know what could or ought to be revealed." *Pride and Prejudice*, chapter 12, Barnes and Noble 1993, p. 148.

friend the truth, the morally immature person would be victim of her fear. The fear and the natural inclination for self-protection would dominate the rational freedom with which she could face this problem squarely. In the case of a morally mature person, the fear would still be present but would lie within the will's sphere of control. Thus I might experience a twinge of fear, and be tempted to resist telling the truth, but I would overcome the influence of fear and deal with the situation rationally and freely. The development of my freedom involves continual integration of aspects and inclinations of my temperament into the totality of my character.

As we saw in chapter four, prudence has an interest in internal as well as external beauty. The beauty of character internal to the will lies within the scope of prudence and is certainly attained by means of an act of internal intuition. This intuition of goodness involves moral motivation: a moral orientation to life. By means of this intuitive act, I am aware of my moral choices as they form a constellation, as they reveal my moral identity. As I am aware of my moral living, prudence enables me to correct and integrate my inclinations around a moral goal: love for God and neighbor. Thus the beauty which prudence seeks to identify and create is internal as well as external.

These aspects of Scotus's presentation highlight his profound contribution to moral discussion, particularly to an understanding of the nature and operation of prudence as practical wisdom. Together the centrality of intuition and the overall aesthetic paradigm provide for a moral discussion where there can be a high level of moral certainty (based on intuitive grasp of objective goodness) without compromising the possibility for error or sin (the will's ability for *non velle*). The immediate relationship to contingent moral data allows for a dynamic understanding of prudential judgment, where the possibility of exceptions to any but the most basic moral principles would be part of the fabric of the moral domain. And, as a type of artistic assessment, prudence is and can be learned, just as any artist must be trained through experience.

A final point of interest is that of objectivity and moral appetite or intuition. In other words, for Scotus, how can I be assured that my appetite is correctly attuned to what is right? The will as rational appetite has two affections: the affection for possession and the affection for justice. While these are not *felt* affections or emotions, they do constitute the rational orientation within each person. The basis for internal self-control is found in the interaction of these two affections within the will. The affection for justice is always operative within the will and seeks to moderate the affection for possession. Together, the two affections provide an initial moral determination for the rational appetite.

Prudence as a Type of Discernment

In his discussion of prudence, Scotus offers a model which might be likened to discernment, for it involves attention to the particular, consideration of moral feelings and affections, integration of aspects of character, knowledge of divine revelation and of general principles and judgment of the best possible course of action to take in a specific situation, all in light of a lifelong journey toward God. As such, his discussion of prudence might offer a fruitful avenue for consideration both by those interested in understanding moral decision-making according to a more integrated model and by those who seek to bring out the riches of the Franciscan tradition today.

The attitude of Francis expressed in the Rule, "you are strangers and pilgrims in this world,"[19] finds its articulation in Scotist thought in the notion of *viator*, or wayfarer. For Scotus, our life in this world is a continuous journey back toward a loving God who has brought us into being and sustains us in gracious liberality. In this way, moral decisions and choices are always made within the context of an entire lifetime of relationship to God and of commitment to following the Gospel.

This relationship and commitment is based upon the highest freedom within the will: that of *firmitas*, or free adherence to another person in love. This sort of freedom is present in God, of course, who loves with an everlasting love. It is less often present, and thus must be cultivated, in us. The distractions of everyday living can diminish the intensity with which we give ourselves to God, or to anyone else for that matter. Thus the human journey requires repeated commitment, on a daily basis, to the spiritual values of the Gospel and to the person of Jesus Christ. There is no "once and for all" commitment after which I can get on about my business of doing other things. A life-long commitment must be dynamic and expressed in living and nurturing life in oneself and in others

---

[19] Later Rule of 1223, chapter 6 in *Francis and Clare: The Complete Works* (Translation and Introduction by Regis J. Armstrong, OFM Cap. and Ignatius C. Brady, OFM), Paulist Press 1982, p. 141.

each day, not the tedious keeping of a promise made long ago to which
one remains faithful, after all love is dead.

Freedom for commitment, or *firmitas*, enables me to dedicate my
life to another person in an ongoing way which is dynamic and which
must inform any decision I make. When I deliberate over a decision, I
cannot do so in isolation from others, but must consider my life as a
whole and in relationship with others. This is particularly significant
within the context of the life of a moral community.

In order to use any information properly in a moral decision, I
must pay attention to my feelings and affections. In Scotus, affections,
while not the highest and most dependable dimension of human rationality, are nonetheless extremely important in the overall decision-
making process. The will itself is constituted by two key affections. In
any act of moral reasoning, these two interact in such a way that they
seek expression in the best possible decision.

Thus human affections are not suspect, nor are they out to derail
rationality in a manner which makes them morally insignificant.
Rather, they provide moral information and seek rational expression.
They do not do this, however, on their own. They are informed by prudence as practical wisdom, which has access to moral principles and to
the concrete situation. Thus for Scotus the moral person seeks ever to
achieve an internal balance between affections for self and for others,
and an external harmony between principles and the demands of the
concrete particular. Quite simply, the entire dynamic resembles a jug-
gling act, and the moral expert is the agile and harmonious artist whose
ability comes after years of training and experience. The image of the
chime returns, only to be personified in the moral expert.

With such concern for the domains of spirituality, general principles, moral affections and the concrete particular, prudence emerges as
a type of discerning faculty. While never ignoring the lessons of moral
norms, the prudent person is not bound in an absolutist manner to follow rules thoughtlessly. However, choices are never made in abstraction
from others, from revelation and from specific information gained
through attention to the particular situation in which one finds oneself.

In addition, the will's native freedom guarantees the value of the
chosen act. No prudential judgment forces the will's assent. The freedom with which the moral person acts grounds the value of the moral
action as entirely within the will's control. In addition, this separation
between the judgment of prudence and the choice within the will

allows for the moment in which a person may act counter to the demands of reason. This moment is present both in the moral expert, for whom such restraint would be error, and in the vicious person, for whom such restraint would be an opportunity for grace. No amount of vicious behavior determines the will to act viciously. The sinner is never totally depraved by past actions or by personal ignorance. The freedom of *non velle* offers the opportunity for grace to intervene in the life of the sinner: it is the moment when conversion is possible. It is true that this moment can derail the intentions of the best person, when failure to act as I should interferes with my moral growth. However, this moment is vital for the possibility of a change of heart.

Scotus calls the prudent person an artist and describes the morally good act as a beautiful whole, expressing harmony of all parts. To achieve this level of moral maturity real training is required. The formative moral community is essential in the development of moral experts who are capable of bringing beauty out of an imperfect world. The perspective of discernment might be an appropriate one in this case, for it provides the communal and spiritual dimensions so evident in Scotist texts. To envision moral decision-making according to a model of discernment may not only provide moral discussion with an alternative thematic, but also scholars within the Franciscan tradition with a method for identifying key elements and values to be enhanced within the discernment process.

Conclusions

A renewed study of Scotus's moral theory (and particularly his presentation of prudence) has significant value for contemporary ethical discussion. First, while he does not rule out errors of perception, Scotus allows for a high level of moral certainty within the judgments of prudence without necessitating acts of choice in the will. This safeguards both the possibility of sin and the enhanced value of the truly well-chosen moral act. Second, Scotus presents moral activity as highly rational and tied to his cognitional theory. This means that the moral agent has direct access via intuition to moral data present in external reality. Such direct access provides information relevant to moral decision making, information which may arise from the affective domain. The contingent realm of choice exhibits objective goodness and beauty to which the moral agent has immediate access.

Third, Scotus integrates the intuitive data with abstract reflection upon principle. This integration highlights the dynamic activity of prudence as that virtue exhibited by the moral expert. She always pays attention to principle, but also seeks to harmonize principle with the specific requirements of concrete situations. Prudence must develop over a lifetime, as principle and virtue seek expression in moral judgment. Scotus does not claim that intuition is a separate moral judgment. Rather, it belongs to the dynamic process of cognition, where acts of abstraction and intuition are united in the operation of prudence.

Fourth, the dynamic moral interaction between scientific (head) and artistic (heart) knowledge results in a moral position which emphasizes both virtue and principle, both character and theory, both intuition and abstraction as key to moral excellence. In addition, this position allows exceptions to occur, and provides for them. Such exceptions do not negate the importance of principle, but rather illustrate how the ideal and real come together in moral reasoning.

Fifth, the presence of moral affections within the will raises the affective domain to a level of importance for any moral decision. My entire experience of being human: my affective, intuitive and abstractive powers provide me with significant moral information for any decision, information which I must seek to integrate and harmonize in light of my entire life as a journey toward God. As such, no decision is isolated from any other in my life.

Finally, Scotus may offer the basis for a theory which transcends a disjunction of virtue and principle. Here is a position which is integrated, which sees moral living as part of a spiritual journey in which training is essential for right appetite, in which principle is important for right judgment, and in which divine aid is never absent in both domains of nature and grace. In his discussion of prudence, Scotus provides a dynamic bridge between the theoretical and practical, whose source is the human desire for goodness and whose goal is the imitation of divine life in creativity. Moral goodness is creativity in the temporal order where conditions are not always perfect. Like Aristotle, Scotus affirms that moral reasoning is a *sui generis* manifestation of rationality, one whose appropriate activity creates character through the informed adjudication of principle.

six

Charity: Mutuality *with* God

Scotus's presentation of moral living and the perfection of human nature culminates in the supreme act of charity: love for God. This act, whereby God becomes my good in friendship, fulfills the movement which began with divine initiative in creation and self-revelation. God's choice to enter into a covenant relationship with humanity is complete with our choice to respond to such infinite goodness and generosity with love and gratitude. Previous aspects of the moral order: the balance of affections, the law revealed in the Decalogue, the harmonious balance of aspects in the morally good act, prudential discernment, all these elements are unified in the act of love for God.

The intricacies of previous chapters come together for us now, as we understand the organic whole of moral living, as parts unite in a single manifestation of beauty. From this vantage point we see the chime as a whole. This whole holds the deepest meaning of human life. For Scotus, *human* means capable of loving, of self-gift and self-revelation to another. Such an activity completes the return to God, from whom all reality takes its source. The circle forms and reality is once again complete. What might have appeared to be fragmented, when considered alone, now takes its place within a larger order, a bigger picture.

Love for God is the highest moral act. By it all other acts are intensified and integrated. Love for God is the natural response of the human heart which continually seeks the good. Friendship with God is that *supernatural* communion which the human heart desires naturally and for which it is naturally constituted. Desired naturally, such friendship can only be achieved by means of the theological virtues of faith, hope and charity. The greatest of these, of course, is charity.

The Theological Virtues

If love for God is the highest moral act of which the will is naturally capable, then how do we achieve it? Which virtue corresponds to it? Do we strive for it or wait for a divine inspiration? It is in Scotus's discussion of this question that we uncover the intricacy of nature and grace at the heart of the Franciscan's vision of human activity. Scotus does not hold that there is a rift between the domain of divine activity and that of human life. There is no sharp contrast between the *natural* and the so-called *supernatural* realms. All reality is one, and divine reality is another dimension beyond our comprehension. Thus, when Scotus explains the meaning of the term *supernatural* in the *Ordinatio* Prologue, he states that it refers to the capacity by which a being achieves its goal. In other words, if the true goal of human flourishing were *natural*, then we could achieve it on our own, just as Aristotle holds in the *Nicomachean Ethics*. However, if the true meaning of human life and flourishing is something we can only achieve in mutuality with God, then it is *supernatural*, that is, beyond our natural powers.[1] Thus, he affirms that we have a natural desire for wholeness which can only be achieved by means of a relationship to God and to others. We are, in fact, the only beings conscious of our need for fulfillment, our need for God. This consciousness motivates moral living.

Scotus integrates the natural and graced dimensions of human existence in his discussion of charity. As a virtue, charity is natural to the human person insofar as the affection for justice informs the activity of choice. When seen within the larger context of a relationship to God, charity enhances the operation of rational freedom by intensifying the activity and focusing the efforts of right loving. Scotus's discussion here reaffirms his commitment to an anthropocentric moral perspective, as he integrates grace into nature and not the contrary.

Earlier discussions of the theological virtues had emphasized the infused character of all virtue. In the 11th century, Hugh of St. Victor and Peter Lombard had tied all virtue to grace as informing moral

---

[1] See Allan Wolter's presentation and discussion of this in "Duns Scotus on the Natural Desire for the Supernatural" in *The Philosophical Theology*, pp. 125-147.

activity. Alan of Lille and Simon of Tournai, in the 12th century, had distinguished the civil from the theological virtues. Charity transforms natural virtue into "catholic virtues". William of Auxerre was responsible for the triumph of the theological definition of virtue in the early 13th century (1225). William defined theological virtue as a good quality by which one lives rightly by means of God's activity within the soul. As gifts from God, theological virtues are infused whereas political virtues are generated through repetition.

Between 1230 and 1250 theologians dealt seriously with the Aristotelian presentation of virtue in the *Nicomachean Ethics*. They would ultimately choose a sharp distinction between theological and philosophical virtues based upon their relationship to the object of their activity. Theological virtues deal with the higher part of the soul and are finalized in God. Philosophical virtues deal with the inferior rational part of the soul and focus on earthly means to the goal. Charity is the "universal mover" for all virtues: love unifies human life with the help of grace. Thinkers in the latter half of the 13th century worked to clarify and systematize this distinction, but there were no drastic departures from the traditional stance in favor of the superiority of theological virtues (faith, hope, charity) over the philosophical (justice, courage, self-control).

Scotus does not alter the basic theological discussion. He does, however, place the virtue of charity within the will as a part of its natural orientation for justice. Scotus removes the intermediate category of infused moral virtues proposed by Aquinas and underscores the natural capacity of the will to love God above all things. Accordingly, human freedom is enhanced by grace, not transformed into a higher nature. Charity functions according to the manner of any virtue: it inclines one toward right loving. Its distinctiveness lies in its object: God. This presentation strengthens the value of human nature and the natural capacity of the will to love the good. It does not theologize all virtue nor does it diminish natural virtue. It still considers charity a primary and necessary part of the human journey toward God. The infused virtue of charity helps the will function more adequately.

Charity, the central theological virtue, is the locus of integration between the spheres of *natural* and *supernatural*. In III, 27 Scotus clearly maintains that love for God is a natural act of which the will is capable, and yet it is charity which intensifies and perfects this act of love. Charity perfects the affection for justice (*affectio justitiae*) within the will, because the command

> to love God above all is an act conformed to natural right reason, which dictates that what is best must be loved most; and hence such an act is right of itself; indeed, as a first practical principle, this is something known *per se*, and hence its rectitude is self-evident. For something must be loved most of all, and it is none other than the highest good, even as this good is recognized by the intellect as that to which we must adhere the most.[2]

The command to love God is a further specification of the first practical principle: "Good is to be loved." As we saw earlier, the affection for justice seeks to love objects according to their worth. In the case of charity we discover a virtue which inclines the will toward the good in the person of God as highest good. Charity is a theological virtue, not because it has a supernatural dimension to its activity, but because its object is God.

> Now, this virtue is theological, because it is directed immediately to a theological object, viz., God. Nor is this all, for this virtue is based immediately upon the first rule of human action, and it had to be infused by God, since this sort of virtue is made to perfect the highest portion of the soul, which cannot be perfected in the best possible way except immediately by God....This virtue which thus perfects the will insofar as it has an affection for justice, I call "charity".[3]

Thus, the human attraction toward rationality and justice reaches its fulfillment only in love. There is only one real moral law: the law of love.

After this clarification of the nature of charity, Scotus discusses the "objective basis" for the act of charity: the formal object of this virtue, that toward which the act of love is directed. Here, he uncovers the intentionality of human love for God. The term "objective basis" refers to the motivation which grounds the act of love. As he explains, the term itself has three meanings. First, it refers to that object which is suited by nature in itself to satisfy the desire expressed in the act. Clearly,

---

[2]   In *Will and Morality*, p. 425.
[3]   In *Will and Morality*, p. 427.

this term applies to God in this fullest sense, for God alone is suited by nature to satisfy the human heart. Thus, God is the only necessary object of love. Second, the term "objective basis" refers to the aspect according to which something is loved. Thus, God is loved according to the degree that the divine nature is self-revealing and perceived as good by those who seek the highest good. This second dimension lies beyond the impersonal notion of infinite goodness: here reciprocity is discovered, God is revealed as a personal being who desires freely to initiate a relationship of friendship.

According to these two meanings of "objective basis" I begin to love God because I recognize that God is infinite goodness. However, this initial love for God is returned and intensified through communion with the divine persons which is the direct result of God's initiative toward me. This relationship of friendship continues to increase in its dynamism which intensifies my subsequent acts of love. God is no longer loved in a theoretical manner, i.e., because of his infinite goodness, but because of the personal self-gift which I now experience.

> For just as in our case someone is first loved honestly, that is, primarily because of himself or herself, and only secondarily because such a one returns our love, so that this reciprocal love in such a person is a special reason of amiability over and above the objective goodness such a person possesses, so too in God. Not only does God's infinite goodness, or his nature as this unique nature in its uniqueness, draw us to love such, but because this "Goodness" loves me, sharing itself with me, therefore I elicit an act of love towards it. And under this second aspect of amiability, one can include everything about God that proves his love for us, whether it be creation or redemption or preparing us for beatitude in heaven...hence he deserves to be loved in return, according to that text from John: "Let us love God because he has first loved us." [4]

The second meaning of "objective basis", then, belongs to the realm of reciprocal relationship or friendship with God. Such personal relationship is "objective" in a manner which might correspond to a more contemporary "inter-subjective" notion, where two subjects are mutually involved in the constitution of "objectivity". This is clearly not the same sort of absolute notion of objective which the first meaning revealed.

[4] In *Will and Morality*, p. 429.

There, it was the divine nature which constituted the objective basis for the exercise of charity. Here, the relationship is intensified through reflection on scripture: God's creative freedom operative in human history. Scripture reveals a key insight: that relationship with God is not something to be earned by human action, but that it is already established by divine gracious liberality. The focus is not my love for God, but God's love for me.

A third and final meaning for "objective basis" refers to the consequences of the activity: what follows or accompanies the act of love for God. This is complete satisfaction of the human desire for God.

> The third meaning refers to the satisfying happiness God gives as our ultimate end, although this is not properly speaking a formal objective reason, since it is a natural consequence of the elicited act of loving him. Nevertheless, inasmuch as this satiety inevitably accompanies this act of love, it could serve as a kind of object. And in this sense God is loved inasmuch as he is that good object that makes us completely happy, and he is said to be loved in this way insofar as he is loved supremely, that is, not *qua* formal object, but under an aspect in the object that accompanies the act of loving it.[5]

Love for God produces consequences within my life: consequences which are measurable. The third meaning of objective refers to the result of personal satisfaction and happiness which offers another reason why I should love God.

There are thus three reasons why the command to love God has an objective basis. First, God is to be loved because of his infinite goodness. In God, "objective" refers to that *per se* nature by which God is the highest good and worthy of the highest love. Second, God is to be loved because "He first loved us." In the relationship to each person, divine love means both the love of God for the person and the love of the person for God. This constitutes the objective (inter-subjective) basis of reciprocal friendship. Finally, God is to be loved because divine infinite goodness satisfies the deepest longing of the human heart. In terms of human desire, there is a "objective" measure for the consequences of an act: happiness or satisfaction. Charity or love for God is not, then, only a subjective act. Reflection upon the act of human love for God reveals three ways in which this act is objectively justified. It is an act whose

---

[5]   In *Will and Morality*, p. 429.

object is infinite goodness, thus worthy of all love. It is an act which is creative of relationship external to the subject. It is an act which produces measurable results.

Scotus concludes this discussion with an example. Not surprisingly, he draws this from the realm of beauty. Assume that there is in nature something which is most beautiful to see. Now, assume that this most beautiful thing were also the source of the eye's power for sight and that vision itself loved such visual beauty. Then, "in seeing this object, the eye's love of seeing was satisfied to the full."[6] The first meaning of "objective basis" refers to the visual beauty, as an adequate object for vision and embodied in something which has all the perfection possible for such beauty. This is *per se* objectivity. The second meaning of "objective basis" represents an additional reason for loving such beauty, insofar as it shares itself with the eye and makes the visual act possible. This is the reciprocal objectivity. The third meaning of "objective basis" points to the fullest satisfaction of the operation of vision. Such is the objectivity measured by consequences.

This discussion of objectivity reveals levels of motivation within the human heart. The primary reason for charity, and thus the purest motivation, is the first or *per se* reason in the divine nature. It is only in this sense that God is the object of the beatific vision. The other two reasons refer to the activity of loving, which is itself enjoyable, but which does not offer the same objective basis for charity. As a theological virtue, charity's primary basis is the divine nature, which can only be known by means of divine self-revelation in Scripture. But charity is not foreign to the natural will and can be understood in the natural context of reciprocal love and satisfaction. The highest motivation and, thus, the fullest expression of charity exist where the will focuses not on itself but on divine goodness and perfection.

It is for this reason that Scotus states that, while the natural will can love the infinite good, the theological virtue of charity is still required for the fullness of human loving. There are two reasons for this. First, in this life, we cannot adequately focus our attention on what we love.

> I say that this precept [to love God above all], both extensively and intensively according to the aforesaid way, can be fulfilled in this life, but not as to all the conditions which are implied by the words "with your whole heart, your whole soul," etc., because in this life

[6]   In *Will and Morality*, p. 429.

there cannot be that recollection of our faculties with all impediments removed, so that the will could exert the sort of effort it could if our powers were all united and recollected and all impediments removed.[7]

Second, human loving does not possess the required intensity for such loving.

> As for the third point of this article, namely, the need for a habit of charity, I reply as I did in that seventeenth distinction of the first book, namely, that this habit adds to the substantial intensity of the act a further intensity, which the will alone could also have given to the act by exerting an equal effort. And the more perfect the created power is, so much more imperfect would it be (speaking arithmetically, for geometrically the imperfection would be equal) if it did not have created charity corresponding to it proportionately.[8]

Here Scotus makes two key points. First, charity adds nothing substantial to the activity of loving that the human heart could not provide on its own. Thus, charity is not supernatural in the sense that it divinizes the human person's activity of loving. Charity increases the intensity of the activity: it adds momentum to what is already moving. Second, when we consider the importance of the human ability for love, we realize that without this added momentum of charity, the will falls far short of its potential. Charity adds focus to the human activity of loving, an activity whose substance is natural.[9]

We might understand this by means of the following example. Imagine someone who would like to carry a load up a slight incline. The load is not too heavy for the person, but it does require some effort. Now imagine a friend who comes to offer help. Her help enables the first person to carry the weight with less effort, even though he would have been able to carry the weight alone. The presence of the second person does not replace the natural ability of the first: it does, however, enhance his ability. The first person is able to perform the activity of

---

7   In *Will and Morality,* p. 441.

8   In *Will and Morality,* p. 441.

9   "As for the substance of the act, however, I maintain what I said there, that the habit is not required." *Will and Morality,* p. 443.

transporting the load with less effort. While the overall result is the same (i.e., the load is moved up the incline) the actual activity is performed more efficiently when two people work together than if one were obliged to complete the task alone. In this way, we see that the presence of charity acts like a friend whose help perfects the natural activity of human loving.

Within this intricate discussion of the influence and necessity of charity for human loving, Scotus never leaves his emphasis on freedom at the center of moral living. No virtue, however valuable, would (or could) direct the self-determination of the free and rational will. To understand how the act of love has both moral (*natural*) and theological (*supernatural*) dimensions, we must reconsider briefly how any virtue affects the will.

From the perspective of free choice, moral virtue is directly related to ordered loving, and is the result of the operation of prudence. As we saw in chapter four, the virtues are proper dispositions for love which intensify the activity of the will. Virtues result from frequent choices and are inclined toward a repetition of similar acts.

> ...therefore since the will is not more determined of itself toward one [act] than the intellect, a certain facility inclining to similar acts can be generated in it by frequently elicited acts, and this I call virtue.[10]

No virtue is separated from the operation of right reason, "...since virtue is an elective practical habit determined by right reason...."[11] Charity, as virtue, is generated by frequent acts of love in light of right reasoning and inclines the will to love with greater generosity. It is the friend who comes to help carry the burden. Like any virtue, charity is an important part of moral living.

It is, however, not the most important part.[12] Just as free choice is morally superior to natural inclination, the will's rational and self-determined activity dominates the discussion of virtue as moral disposition in Scotus's presentation of the moral dynamic. This is not surprising, since

[10]   III, 33, unica, n. 5, (Vivès 15:442b).

[11]   *Collationes,* I, n. 11 (Vivès 5:137b).

[12]   "For Duns Scotus, just as for St. Augustine, virtue is not something valuable simply because it is a way of acting that is measured by, and in accordance with, nature, as Aristotle teaches, but because of the act of love by which the virtuous act is directed to God." Bettoni, *Duns Scotus: Basic Principles of his Philosophy,* CUP 1961, p. 169.

the virtues possess a natural quality, insofar as they are the product of repetition and can become unreflective habits.

For example, I might be a person who is naturally generous and for whom it is difficult to say no to any request. Over the years, I develop this pattern to such an extent that it becomes *automatic*, in the sense that I no longer reflect upon my responses, but rather acquiesce immediately. This is not necessarily questionable; however, it is not as good as conscious reflection and choice of response in any situation. Scotus holds, quite simply, that it is better to respond with reflection than merely respond. This does not mean that every human decision has to be accompanied by intense scrutiny. Rather, it means that when I act with knowledge I am expressing my humanity in a way which differentiates me from an automaton. Since virtue is not the central element in Scotus's vision, the moral virtues (justice, courage, temperance) are not necessarily related to one another,[13] but are each related to prudence. Thus, one may possess a single virtue in the absence of any one of the others, just as one may possess one of the five senses without another.

> While virtue is a perfection of man, it does not represent complete perfection, for then one moral virtue would suffice. But when something has several partial perfections, it can be simply perfect according to one perfection and simply imperfect according to another, as is apparent in the case of man, who has many organic perfections and can have one in the highest degree and not have another. For example, someone may be disposed in the highest way as to sight and touch but lack any hearing. Someone can possess the highest degree of perfection in matters of temperance and not have the perfection required as regards another perfection....[14]

There is no natural or necessary connection among the virtues; there is, however, a necessary connection of each to prudence, as right reasoning.

The theological virtues (faith, hope and charity) belong to a superior order, since they are infused and not acquired. Charity perfects the

---

[13] Borak, in "Libertà e prudenza nel pensiero di Duns Scoto" (*Laurentianum* 10 (1969), 105-141), claims that Scotus cares more about the person who has virtues than about the interconnection of the virtues themselves.

[14] *Ordinatio* III, suppl. d. 36, revised with Codices A and S in *Will and Morality*, p. 389.

highest nature of the will (*affectio justitiae*), hope perfects the affection for possession (*affectio commodi*) and faith perfects prudence. All three virtues direct their respective activity to God. Thus, the theological virtues relate to the *object* of the affections (external dynamic) and the moral virtues perfect the *exercise* of the affections (internal dynamic).[15] The theological virtues finalize the activity of human loving, since they are directed toward God alone, infinite goodness and the ultimate object of all love.

The virtues which focus on God help to integrate the internal and external domains of human activity. The internal discussion of the exercise of right loving focuses on natural or acquired virtues which are born within the will and develop by means of right action. The external discussion of love for God shifts the attention from the moral person to the entire context within which this person exists and acts. It also underscores the objective basis for moral action. An act done out of love for God possesses a larger domain, a broader context than one done out of self-interest. The example of almsgiving clarifies this point. I might give to the poor to enhance my reputation. Here the context is narrow, for I am only thinking of myself. However, if I were to give out of concern or compassion for the poor, or out of love for God, I would expand my moral universe to include greater and greater dimensions. To focus all my actions on the ultimate object of all love is to expand my moral horizons as far as possible and to unite all my actions under one concern. Such focus integrates my life around a common theme and expresses a common value. No act, no choice is irrelevant. Every movement of my life contributes to the intensity and integration which I bring to the world around me.

The virtues, whether moral or theological, intensify the activity of the will. As the discussion in chapter four clarified, virtues do not replace human freedom as central moral element but rather increase the ability of the person to choose and act properly. Scotus explains this relationship clearly in *Ordinatio* I, 17:

> However, it [the will] works less perfectly without the practical habit [virtue] than with it (and this granted equal effort on the part of the will) as when two causes concur toward one effect, one alone cannot by itself [cause] the effect as perfectly as the two can together. And in this way [the position] is saved whereby the act is more

[15] III, 26, unica, n. 18 (Vivès 15:341a).

intense [*intensior*] coming from the will and virtue than from the will alone... because two concurring causes can produce a more perfect effect than either one alone, —which effect however in itself is a whole and *per se* one from two causes, but in diverse relations to the causes.[16]

Here he explains simply the influence of any virtue upon the moral act. This explanation takes the form of a causal analysis, where he examines the double order (natural and free) which produces the moral act. Together, natural and free choice produce moral excellence, since the fullest perfection of the moral act requires both the choice of rational freedom and the influence of natural disposition.[17] Virtue, habitual excellence, is a disposition toward goodness developed over time and in accord with moral reasoning. The virtues offer that natural, habitual facility which enhances the will's ability to make the right moral choices.

As we have seen, Scotus holds that, while virtue does not replace the will as central moral element, an act performed solely "by the will" in the presence of no natural inclination or disposition would be less perfect than one performed both freely (through the will) and naturally (through virtue).[18] The moral act is one, yet it has two separate relationships: to the will and to virtue. The moral order does not exist independently from the natural. As we saw in the treatment of the will itself and of moral goodness, Scotus nowhere identifies a "purely moral" dimension within the will which does not somehow rely upon what is natural. This does not, however, prevent the will from acting freely, and thus in a way which might, at times, run counter to natural inclination. To say

[16] I, 17, n. 40 (5:154).

[17] Wolter's discussion is especially enlightening here, as he elaborates on Scotus's reference to geometric and arithmetic proportional increases: "Suppose for example, the natural capacity is doubled; then a will capable of loving naturally with an intensity of only two will be able to love with an intensity of four, whereas a more perfect will capable of loving naturally with an intensity of eight will be able, with charity, to love with an intensity of sixteen.... Hence, speaking simply or in an unqualified sense, the more perfect the will's natural capacity to love God is, the more it has to gain by having charity." Wolter, *Will and Morality*, pp. 93-4.

[18] "Briefly, then, I say, as I said there [in I,17] the reason habits are needed because of acts, especially the act of charity, is due to something that is a circumstance of the act. As for the substance of the act, however, I maintain what I said there, that the habit is not required." III, 27 in *Will and Morality*, p. 443.

the will functions freely is not to say that it is totally separated from natural dispositions.

To return to our example of almsgiving, we can imagine two distinct scenarios. The first, where I give to the poor to enhance my reputation, expresses an act which is freely chosen but not in the presence of virtue, either natural or theological. My motivation is self-interest (*affectio commodi*), even though the act of almsgiving is a good act. Since I have chosen this act freely, I can be praised for it, but if everyone knew my motivation they would not praise me very much.

The second scenario shows me offering alms out of compassion for the poor or out of love for God. The act looks the same from the outside, but is actually entirely different. Here, my motivation is influenced by the natural affection for justice, the moral virtue of prudence and the theological virtue of charity. This act is superior to the first insofar as my motivation integrates it into a broad context unified by love. However, in the act of giving to the poor, even with all the high motivation I may have, I am still conscious that I might have chosen to act otherwise, to refrain from generosity or to turn away and not notice the person in need. This consciousness indicates the independence of the will *even in the performance of a good action*. No matter how good my actions are, I am always aware of my freedom to do otherwise. This consciousness of freedom does not exist prior to my choice, but actually accompanies my choice and is an immanent indication of the freedom within me. Thus, the will continues to function freely even in the presence of high moral and theological dispositions which enhance the exercise of choice.

The Order of Meritorious Goodness

The moral realm is not the highest order of human goodness. The relationship with God which mutual love creates gives birth to the order of merit, or meritorious goodness. This is that level at which divine and human relationships intersect within the good act. Scotus defines the dimension of merit as that whereby the human moral act is "accepted by the divine will relative to a reward, or its acceptability or worthiness of acceptance." [19] The order of merit does not exist alone within an act, but, like moral goodness, depends upon the prior existence of lesser orders: natural, virtuous and charitable. Thus, an act enters the dimension of

[19]   *Lectura* I, 17, n. 142 (17:226).

merit when it is good, freely chosen in light of right reasoning and done out of love. Merit belongs to the act when it is accepted and rewarded by God.

Just as the moral order depends upon the natural, so too does it relate closely with the higher order of merit, whose primary virtue is charity. Love for God is, of course, the supreme virtue and goal of the moral life. In contrast to hope, which is directed to the perfection (in God) of the desire for gain or satisfaction (*affectio commodi*), charity seeks no personal reward. In charity there is no trace of selfish love or concupiscence. Charity increases the natural capacity of the will to love God not as a personal good but as that infinite good which alone is worthy of absolute love.[20]

In *Ordinatio* I, 17 Scotus discusses the mutual interaction of charity and freedom within the meritorious order. Charity is a virtue (indeed, it is the highest virtue) and as such never forces the will to choose. Rather, it accompanies the will's choice and facilitates correct choice through proper intentionality. Simply put, to perform an act out of love is easier than to perform it out of a sense of duty or under constraint. While charity functions as a secondary factor in the moral order, it takes primary place in the order of merit. Charity is the principal condition for merit; it defines the order of acceptance:

> ...for the act is more accepted as worthy of the reward because it is elicited by charity than because it is freely chosen by the will, although both are necessarily required.[21]

Two examples clarify the relationship of mutuality between choice and love here. The first is taken from music and the relation of harmony to the audience.

> Likewise, sound comes more from percussion of a sounding body than from the order of percussion and yet (as acceptable to the sense of hearing) it is more from the order of percussion than from the power causing the sound; indeed if it is not an harmonic sound, it is totally unacceptable to the sense of hearing.[22]

[20] "This virtue which thus perfects the will insofar as it has an affection for justice, I call charity." *Will and Morality*, p. 427.
[21] *Ordinatio* I, 17, n. 152 (5:211).
[22] I, 17, n. 152 (5:211).

Thus, when I pluck the strings of a guitar or play the piano, the sound originates from the activity of striking the chord. Sound comes from a sounding body (string or key), just as moral acts come from the free act of choice in the will. Whether the sound is harmonious or dissonant, however, does not come from striking the chord or key, but rather from the relationships between the chords (keys) and from the nature of harmony, which is the purpose of music. Likewise, the meritorious quality of an act comes not from the will which is its source but from the relation of the act to its end or purpose and from the harmonic relationship of all aspects. An act which is freely chosen is still incomplete, for it has not been finalized or directed toward the goal of all human activity: love.

The second example is that of the mutuality between mother and father in the birth of a child. The father may be the principal cause for generation, but the mother is principal cause insofar as the child experiences love and acceptance. Thus, from one point of view, the father looks like the most important factor in procreation. But from another, and higher, perspective, it is actually the mother who is most important.

> ...if the father is principal cause of the son and the mother less principal, yet she can be more principal cause of the son, insofar as the child is loved or experiences being loved by someone, so that the child is loved more because of the mother who bore him, than because of the father who generated him.[23]

Scotus moves here between two perspectives: source and completion. The primary cause of the child's life is the father's impregnation of the mother, just as the primary cause of the moral act is the free choice of the will. However, this is only one perspective. From another vantage point, the child will never thrive without the experience of maternal love and nurturing. Thus, the moral act never reaches completion without love. A free act is an incomplete act. Love alone can bring it to completion. God's *acceptatio* functions in this passage as the activity of divine maternal love, since it is by this love that the human act is completed and brought to fulfillment.

A final aspect of the meritorious order is the manner in which charity actually makes the object loved present to the lover, and thus unites lover with beloved. Here we discover again the preference for love over knowledge at the heart of moral living. When I know something, I "take

---

[23] I, 17, n. 152 (5:211).

it in" and can only known it according to my mental ability. It becomes part of me and is subject to my biases and my personal point of view. Knowledge "duplicates" the object within me. The act of loving, on the other hand, takes me out of myself and joins me to the beloved in a way which transforms me into what I love. Charity joins me, unites me to God in a manner which far surpasses any knowledge of God I might have. In charity we all have equal access to God and are divinized by the relationship of love. The order of charity is an order of transformation into God, of fulfillment and nurturing so that we become whole. Charity continues the moral dynamic and fosters growth and develop-ment, so that the act performed out of charity brings goodness to birth in the person and in the world.

Divine Acceptance

As formal object of the act of charity, God also responds to human love, creating a bond of reciprocity and satisfaction. This is the bond of friendship (*amor amicitiae*), that state of mutuality in which a person loves God with her whole heart and is loved in return. Consciousness of this friendship produces delight, which, while not being the motivation for the relationship, always accompanies it. Friendship with God is, then, the highest human activity and the goal of the moral life.[24] Christian love is best expressed in that love of friendship which looks beyond selfish interests toward the good of the other. Thus the goal of all moral action is an act of selfless love, totally determined by the value of the beloved. This is the perfection of affection for justice.

> First I say that charity...is called that practical habit by which God is held dear. ...since God, who is common good, does not wish to be anyone's per-sonal good... therefore, God, infusing the habit by which the soul moves orderly and perfectly toward him, gives the habit by which he is held dear, as common good and to be loved jointly by others...[25]

Here we see how love is creative of the moral community. God is "com-mon good" and does not wish to belong to any one person alone. It belongs to the divine nature to initiate a community of co-lovers. The perfection of justice in love flows beyond any one individual's friend-

---

[24] Scotus's development of this position relies heavily upon Aristotle's discussion in Books 8 and 9 of the *Nicomachean Ethics.*

[25] *Ordinatio* III, 28, unica (Vivès 15:378b).

ship with God and moves toward a common, inclusive reality. Salvation is not merely a personal, individual experience. The dynamic of charity grows and expands to create a community of all persons. The other-centered quality of the affection for justice never turns back to become an affection for possession, but intensifies its activity in view of bringing all to a better understanding of the goodness of God. Like the Trinity, communion with God pours forth a love which creates relationship within reality. Charity introduces the lover into a genuine participation in divine life.

Within the moral dimension of human activity, the theological virtue of charity never threatens the will's primacy. What natural reason commands (love for the highest good) charity intensifies (love for God alone). In this manner charity specifies the will's love for God as its object and introduces the will into the order of merit. Here again we discover an active/passive balance, as my action inspired by charity must "await" divine response. I can only be disposed to reward. "...but the completion of merit is only in my dispositive power, which is always followed by a divine disposition to act for the completion of my act...."[26] The balance Scotus strikes here is delicate, as the Franciscan moves from human action to divine response in an effort to maintain the value and importance of both. Merit is the function of acceptance (on God's part) of an act (of mine) which is harmonious. Scotus does not see merit as an order which transforms the act, for merit neither changes nor does it perfect the act ("I deny that it is a more perfect reality"). The act itself has the harmony of goodness which results from mutuality at all levels, both natural and free. The reward given by God's acceptance adds nothing to the act itself. Rather, it places the act within a relationship to infinite reward.

No human act is ever ordered *per se* toward the ultimate reward of beatitude, or eternal life with God. Only divine justice is capable of conferring such a reward upon the human person. God's acceptance, like the free act of the human will, is never the necessary result of good actions. It is rather the free gift of divine love. Scotus describes divine acceptance as the exercise of liberality and admits that God rewards far beyond what any human act deserves. Thus divine "justice" is beyond justice strictly speaking, because God never gives us what we deserve, but rather far beyond anything we could hope to receive. The order of

[26] I, 17, n. 146 (5:209).

merit possesses an unknown dimension, one of divine goodness which
is ordered from all eternity and easily forgoes the demands of strict justice. The divine response to human moral living is as unknowable as it is
generous.

Despite what we cannot know of God's intention to reward us for
our efforts to love, natural reason can, with the help of revelation, work
out some of the eternal plan of God.

> ... it must be known that [it is] by an eternal divine acceptance, by
> which God, from all eternity, seeing such an act chosen from such
> principles, has willed to ordain it to such a reward, its merit. When
> considered accordingly by such divine acceptance, this act would
> not be worthy of its reward according to a notion of strict justice.
> This is proven because the reward is always greater than the good
> in the act which merits, and strict justice can never render a greater
> reward for a lesser good. And so, it is well said that God always
> rewards beyond our worth, and universally beyond any particular
> value which an act might merit. This merit is beyond nature and its
> intrinsic goodness, it is from a gratuitous divine acceptance; and
> even more, beyond that justice which would commonly reward an
> act, for God rewards by means of pure liberality.[27]

Scotus continues his unflagging optimism as he focuses attention on
the dynamic cosmic return of all things to God, a return which is
enhanced by human moral cooperation. In this person-centered perspective reminiscent of 12th century spirituality, the Franciscan por-
trays God as a Trinity of Persons who exercise generous liberality in
response to human efforts. Divine justice does not have the final word,
divine generosity does.

The meritorious order transcends the moral, as divine liberality
rewards the charitable act. Every moral act is thus potentially meritorious, given proper motivation. The virtue of charity lies at the frontier
between the orders of morality and merit. Love for God alone is within
the capacity of the natural will, and yet the intensity of love for God is
increased with the presence of charity as infused inclination. In the
order of merit, divine love comes to meet the human heart and joins it
in its activity.

Meritorious perfection is the fulfillment of the moral order. Here
the will's highest motivation is rewarded as it enters into a intensified

[27]   I, 17, n. 149 (5:210).

personal dynamic of friendship with God, no longer seen as "infinite goodness" but as this very personal being, whose essence is selfless love and who wills to be in relationship with all. Thus the moral order perfects internal motivation while the meritorious finalizes the moral act by creating a relationship with God.

Conclusion

Scotus culminates his discussion of the moral domain from the divine viewpoint. The process which began within the human heart as a dynamic interchange between two affections develops by means of natural inclinations and rational reflection. Charity unifies the entire movement of the will toward the good, as this theological virtue focuses the will's activity on the highest and most perfectly good person, God.

Mutuality functions fully at this important point, with the divine response to human activity in the order of merit. And, typical of divine activity, this response far exceeds any human effort. "Eye has not seen, nor has ear heard, nor can the mind conceive what God has prepared for those who love..." (1 Cor. 2:9). Human moral activity and development culminate in an activity centered on God and with God. This divinization which awaits us defies philosophical conjecture. Like the human will, the divine will functions out of freedom and reveals itself in gracious generosity.

From this perspective, the earlier stages of moral discussion form a unity which integrates character and choices throughout a lifetime. Both intentionally and extensionally, the activity of rational human loving integrates the human person and promotes the mutuality of communion with others and with God. The completed journey transcends any concept we might have of it.

The wind chime dances gracefully in the breeze and pours forth its harmonic song for all to hear. Both as moral living and as moral person, the chime offers an image of the goal of human life: to delight God with the music we are able to make. Our chime is cause for divine rejoicing; our hearts are filled with a delight of divine origin. This final union and communion fills the garden with harmonic peace and joins in the song of all creation to praise the generosity of a loving God who calls us forth to join together in the cosmic dance of love.

seven

The Harmony of Goodness

In this final chapter we reprise the elements of Scotus's moral vision and reflect upon its significance for contemporary ethical discussion. It does little good to examine the thoughts of the past if we do not consider how they might influence present-day concerns. At the outset of this study, I indicated that it is not possible to transplant Scotist thought into the late 20th century. The more modest goal which has informed our efforts is that of a dialogue with the mind of this great Franciscan thinker. This has been difficult insofar as his works are not yet totally available in critical form. Despite the difficulties presented by the textual evidence, it has been possible to present and clarify key insights from this intricate and subtle "unravelling" of reality typical of Scotus. These insights have stretched from a precise analysis of the composition of the individual in *haecceitas*, through the central element of freedom which undergirds all reality, to a communion with the divine in the order of merit. From the most delicate detail to the greatest grasp of cosmic order, the mind of Scotus seeks to place everything exactly where it belongs within an essential order which unites God and all creation.

In his philosophical and theological reflections, Scotus has great concern for detail and precision. This is evident in the power of his analytic mind and logical rigor. While most scholarly studies highlight these elements, few call attention to his concern for integration. This aspect is perhaps even more important than the value of his analytic gifts. For Scotus, the intricate parts form a glorious whole, just as the myriad bits of colored glass join together in forming the beautiful stained-glass windows in medieval cathedrals. The vision of the whole does not negate the beauty of the parts, but brings various colors, shapes and sizes into harmonic relationship. I have chosen to call this related-ness "mutuality" because it exists to an eminent degree among persons. Although all reality is part of a relational order, person-based mutuality is a free relationship, entered into out of love and self-gift. It is proper to the divine reality of the Trinitarian mystery and the goal of human moral living. Scotus's profound insights demonstrate not only analytic, but synthetic gifts as well.

Throughout this present study we have seen that the Subtle Doctor does not offer a precise or step-by-step method for moral decisions. He offers, rather, a presentation of moral living and moral elements which constitute a paradigm focused on beauty and harmony. This presenta-tion is centered around love, and thus, around the will as a free, rational potency. The will reaches out toward all that is good and works to bal-ance concerns for self with objective values. The dynamic process of rational loving involves natural dispositions toward goodness and divine assistance in grace. The manner in which Scotus discusses moral living and his efforts toward the integration of nature and grace into a work of art suggest that he would be a significant partner in any moral dialogue. As we conclude, it is appropriate to review thematically the key aspects which stand out as important qualities of Scotist thinking: the aesthetic integration of goodness and beauty, the centrality of love and the will in moral discussion, the goods of balance and harmony for human flourishing, the integrity of rational loving and the primacy of mutuality for moral living.

The Aesthetic Integration

Beauty has only recently re-entered the philosophical discussion as a serious element. Umberto Eco's works on Aquinas's aesthetic theories continue to influence a renaissance of scholarship on medieval thinkers and particularly in light of theories of beauty.[1] Jan Aertsen examines the importance of aesthetic concerns in his recent article "Beauty in the Middle Ages: A Forgotten Transcendental?"[2] Aertsen focuses on Thomas Aquinas and underscores the importance of the

[1]   Umberto Eco, *Art and Beauty in the Middle Ages*, Yale University Press 1986 and *The Aesthetics of Thomas Aquinas*, Harvard University Press 1989.
[2]   *Medieval Philosophy and Theology*, vol. 1 (1991), pp. 68-97.

integration of beauty with truth and goodness for the medieval mind. Beauty was not seen to be a separate transcendental but part of an over-all "integrated sensibility" of medieval experience.[3] Francis Kovach studies the importance of beauty for Aquinas and Scotus in his several articles.[4]

Beyond the specifically medieval relevance of a theory of beauty, Martha Nussbaum's *The Fragility of Goodness* [5] overtly links the notions of moral goodness with beauty. Hans Urs von Balthasar's *The Glory of the Lord* seeks to begin a discussion on a "theological aesthetics." Von Balthasar maintains that a loss of the notion of beauty as a significant transcendental results in the loss of the other transcendentals: truth and goodness.[6] The centrality of beauty in moral discussion for classical thinkers simply cannot be ignored in a contemporary search for a renewed moral framework. The desire for wholeness which typifies the best of medieval thinking offers another model for our culture frag-mented by divisions and disputes. Our age has been named Post-Modern, Post-Christian, Post-Value. We watch the breakdown of the social and political order around the world and experience the impact of world events on our understanding of reality. There is no longer a coherent worldview in this post-Cold War era.

Scotus and medieval thinkers like him rise above partial perspec-tives to offer an understanding of moral living which is closely related to a spirituality of goodness and love, which integrates the partial view-points into an organic and dynamic description of human living, and which does not seek to oversimplify the intricacies within reality. Moral

---

[3] "The aesthetic is not in the Middle Ages an autonomous domain alongside the true and the good. The integration of the beautiful with other values did not need to be based on a distinct transcendental: it was implied in the transcendental order of truth and goodness." Aertsen, "Beauty in the Middle Ages...", p. 97.

[4] See his several articles in *Scholastic Challenges to Some Mediaeval and Modern Ideas,* 1987.

[5] Cambridge University Press 1987.

[6] "In a world without beauty — even if people cannot dispense with the word and constantly have it on the tip of their tongues in order to abuse it — in a world which is perhaps not wholly without beauty, but which can no longer see it or reckon with it: in such a world the good also loses its attractiveness, the self-evidence of why it must be carried out. Man stands before the good and asks himself why it must be done and not rather its alternative, evil." *The Glory of the Lord,* San Francisco: Ignatius Press 1989, p. 19.

living is not a mathematical problem nor a technological calculus; it is the human response to the events of life. As a model of integration, Scotus's moral vision offers several values which make it attractive today.

This vision is optimistic about human nature. In the will's two affections we find a straightforward description of the desires within the human heart. Not only do we possess a desire for justice but also a healthy desire for self-protection. The human will is constituted so as to respond rationally to the command of Jesus: love your neighbor as yourself. Both love of self and love of neighbor are required in moral living; their proper relationship of mutuality must be the result of rational deliberation and choice. In developing his insights, Scotus drew from the legacy of 12th century anthropocentric moral reflection and integrated this perspective into his profound understanding of Aristotle's ethical theory.

Within the constitution of the will lies the key to self-control. The moral dimension is a natural one, one which expresses the best within human nature. Human choices in light of self and others move naturally toward ordered and rational consistency, if there is a moral community to support such choices. The natural affections of the human heart are able to develop toward increasingly higher levels of moral awareness in a society where good is rewarded and evil punished.

The will and its affections do not exist in a vacuum. Scotus's vision is also extremely optimistic about the goodness found throughout reality. The insight of St. Francis about our connectedness to all nature informs Scotus's moral understanding. All reality is good and beautiful. That is why for Scotus moral loving does not so much involve finding those objects worthy of love (since all reality is good), but rather working out the intricate manner by which to love reality as it ought to be loved. My moral living involves my relationship to reality around me and my efforts to strengthen and enhance that mutuality.

The value of relationship imbues the entire perspective. Since all reality is good, then my relationships with others and with creation ought to promote goodness. In addition, my relationship with God becomes a key part of my moral living and my moral choices. My goal in life centers around the proper integration of all aspects of reality. I enter the dynamic process of divinization by bringing all segments of my life into a whole, both intentionally through charity and extensionally throughout my lifetime. The final goal is not a state of "eternal rest" but rather an eternal dynamic life of mutuality, part of a giant cosmic return of all things to God. The integration of grace and nature in Scotus's presentation underscores the presence and activity of God at all levels of human living.

Spirituality forms the background against which Scotus speaks of moral living. Although the law offers objective basis for right action, this does not form the basis for an obligational moral scheme. Rather, the law supports a moral dynamic where friendship with God and with nature unify all aspects of life. This spirituality is trinitarian and, thus, specifically Christian. This is not to say that Scotist thought would not be attractive to non-Christians, for it acknowledges the goodness of the world and its relation to God. In the journey of human life, all reality moves toward fullness, toward union with the divine. As human members of this journey, we can, by our choices, prevent or promote this ultimate union.

This vision is dynamic and organic. All reality, human and natural, grows toward the future. Today new levels of consciousness promote the integration of all aspects into one reality, the "global village" or "spaceship earth" motifs. Moral living is also dynamic and organic, and moral choices promote life and growth, flourishing and development. The promotion of moral attitudes and of fully-developed moral character belongs not only to each individual but to families and moral communities. The seed of practical reasoning must be nourished so that it might grow and develop into the excellence of practical wisdom which exists in the artisan of character, completely developed in the perfection of love.

Scotus's presentation of moral goodness as beauty has a great deal to offer contemporary reflection upon ethical living. Together with his description of the judgment of prudence as artistic discernment, his vision of the moral as beautiful integrates once more the domains of goodness and beauty, of moral living and art. The artistic image is a dynamic representation of the activity proper to rationality: creativity. This creativity expresses the image of God within each person as well as the individual beauty each one holds as proper identity. The artist who creates speaks himself in his creation. The moral artist who acts speaks herself in her activity. Scotus overtly joins the two domains of moral and artistic theory in a manner which demands far more attention than I have been able to give in this short work. A great deal more historical study needs to be done, especially in terms of the history of music theory in medieval culture.

An extremely attractive aspect of the aesthetic dimension of Scotist thought is his use of musical imagery. The musical images bring together the divine and human wills, as the divine ear delights in the actions of the human heart inspired by charity. The harmony which exists within the human heart but also in the activities of loving cannot fail to reach the divine listener. God's attention to human living is not a distant, detached, objective observer but a listening presence who initiated the dialogue long ago in the desert of Sinai. God spoke to Moses, to the people of Israel and revealed the relationship of being which unites us and all reality to God as loving Creator, Redeemer and Sanctifier. God has not left this attitude of relatedness but continues to lend an ear to the cries of the human heart and especially to the cries of the poor.

As exemplar for all human living, God does not simply listen to human concerns, but also responds quickly with salvific action and generous grace. The specific discussion of prudence as moral discernment captures the human response to such divine exemplarity. Like God, the mature moral agent acts quickly to do what should be done. This activity unites character and principle perspectives into a single focus. This is extremely important for the resolution of the debate which appears to juxtapose the domains of virtue and principle as two different ways of moral thinking. Scotus would agree that they are two different perspectives, but he would deny their juxtaposition. In the presentation and operation of prudence, we discover the fundamental unity of virtue with principle. The discussion of prudence casts the moral decision-making process in a new light. Moral certainty takes into account the specific nature of moral reasoning. It is neither absolutely scientific nor is it completely relative to culture. The mature moral expert possesses that quality of mind and heart whereby she is able to discern the proper course of action in light of fundamental moral principles and the requirements of a particular moral situation.

Scotus presents a portrait of moral living which contributes significantly to contemporary moral discussion. He struggles to harmonize the best of Aristotelian thinking with Christianity,[7] especially within the

---

[7]   Borak maintains that it was the Christian notion of *imago Dei* which provided a more perfect depiction of human nature as a spiritual reality, and thus enabled

Augustinian tradition. In this way, his discussion deals both with objective goodness and its foundation (in God) and with the subjective realm of human moral choice. While highlighting the will's freedom, he does not endow the finite will with the authority to create goodness. While emphasizing the role of right reason, he refuses to maintain a position which dismisses natural inclination as morally insignificant. The will is naturally and rationally constituted to achieve moral excellence.

The Centrality of Love and the Will

Scotus's choice to organize moral elements around the will and, thus, to place love at the core of the moral life has several interesting implications for contemporary moral discussion. Perhaps most important among these is the fact that, for Scotus, the moral order is a relational order. Not only is the will related to the highest good as its object, and to rationality, but the functioning of this relational order produces an ethic of mutuality whose moral goal is friendship with God and whose exemplar is the Trinity.

The source of this dynamic for friendship is the will with its two affections for justice and possession. These enable the will to control its movement by means of the rationality which belongs to any free cause capable of self-direction. The Scotist emphasis upon the will at the heart of moral living reflects his preference for loving God rather than knowing God, although he would never deny the value of the intellectual ascent. If, however, truth about God does not result in greater love for him, then the intellectual achievement counts for no more than straw. The journey of the human will and the human heart finds its completion in love for that Trinity of persons who is infinite goodness. Only a relationship of love with God satisfies the deepest human longing. Such deep human satisfaction is intensified when the relation becomes mutual in divine response.

Scotus underscores the centrality of *praxis* as moral activity in the will. The domain of practical reasoning is determined in light of the natural potential of the will to enter into relationships freely, relationships which are good and life producing. The freedom within the will's affec-

---

Scotus to accept Aristotle's definition of "rational animal" and reject any determinism or intellectualism in favor of freedom. See his "Libertà e prudenza nel pensiero di Duns Scoto" in *Laurentianum*, 10 (1969), p. 105.

tions is purified throughout a lifetime, as experience gives rise to better and better choices. The intellect aids the will in this process of purification, as prudence helps the will to function in light of practical principles and the demands of concrete situations. The goal of moral living is not reward, but the proper functioning of a will inspired by love and divine friendship. The moral will seeks to love God above all things, and for God alone, not because of any reward promised by God. For this reason, Scotus places his discussion of reward in the order of merit, itself a theological dimension of the human journey. The philosophical domain deals with the appropriate moral action on moral grounds alone and not on the basis of any information found in Scripture.

The passage from the moral to meritorious order is made possible by the virtue of charity, natural to the will. This theological virtue of love is the delicate bridge between human and divine realities. It is the point of contact between God and the human person, for it joins both the demands of rational principle and the longing of the heart. In addition, the divine response to human charity infuses and intensifies human choices. Together the human and divine wills function together. The goal of moral *praxis*, then, is relational activity guided by reason. This relational activity is not limited to the human domain but includes the divine as merit crowns the moral order with divine delight.

The experience of friendship with God creates an expanding dynamic of inclusivity. Love for God does not exclude love for self and others. Love for God does not reduce God to the status of personal property. Love for God intensifies and generates love for others; it creates communion. Consciousness of the reciprocal relationships proper to such communion with God and others produces delight within the will, as it experiences moral excellence. Joy, then, is the hallmark of the truly moral agent. The order of merit does not result in moral righteousness but in gratitude to divine mercy which extends beyond any requirements of justice. The person who has attained such a goal is one who knows how to perceive and appreciate beauty in reality and in others. Such a person stands in awe and wonder at reality around him.

With mutuality, joy and friendship as the moral goal, there is no sense in which true moral excellence can be considered an individual effort or achievement. The moral person is always in relation to goodness, to God, to others. Scotus advocates an other-centered moral dynamic: love motivated by the value of the other, love culminating in self-sacrifice for the other. This moral goal creates a community where each member seeks the good of all. The fullest expression of moral life is relationship to others, not in manipulation or control, but in respect and love.

Here, then, is no individualized moral vision based upon obligation as primary motivation but upon a love which rationally seeks to respond appropriately to the goodness that manifests itself in each being and to extend membership in the moral community to all. It is a particularly Christian ethical vision where love for God takes pride of place but does not exclude love for self or for others. In imitation both of Trinitarian mutuality and Incarnational selflessness, human moral action is that action whereby persons enter into the dynamic of divinity. In this moral universe, there are only persons in relationship.

Moral living begins with the rational perception of goodness. It develops through the interaction of the desire for possession and the desire to love justly. Its culmination is that mutuality characteristic of friendship, where each person seeks the good of another and experiences profound delight. The moral goal is a work of art, harmonized both internally (in the will's operation) and externally (in the performance of moral actions).

Balance and Harmony: The Wind Chime

In the introduction, I suggested an image for Scotist moral discussion: the wind chime. I chose this image because it combines elements of balance and harmony with dimensions of visual and musical beauty. I maintain that in Scotus we find an intricate presentation of moral goodness which is dynamic and which requires the development of artistic character which is capable of a discerning judgment about what ought to be done. While each chapter has focused on an aspect of the chime, it is important to reprise all aspects in a final discussion.

As we have seen, the chime is composed of several individual pieces which, while separate from one another, must hang in an appropriate relationship to each other in order for the chime to sound. This images the foundational insight of Scotus that each person is an individual in relationship. *Haecceitas* is not an independent reality, if by independent one means totally separated from all others. The Trinity exemplifies this person-in-relationship and functions as personal goal for all human living. It is communion, not autonomy, which lies at the end of the moral journey. The chime must exhibit balance of all elements. This balance does not require a one to one correlation, however. Two smaller pieces may very well balance a larger piece. The point is that the entire configuration be balanced.

Every chime requires a center disk which is sufficiently weighted to hang appropriately yet sufficiently light to be moved by the wind. The will is such a central element, weighted by its two affections for justice and for possession, yet free enough to move toward the surrounding pieces. Of course, here the wind chime imagery falls short, for in Scotus the will is a rational self-mover and not moved by anything else in a strong sense of determinism. Yet the disk is at the center of other pieces, just as the will functions within a given context. A discussion of the freedom of the will in the absence of any choice makes no more sense than a discussion of a wind chime composed only of a disk hanging from a string with no other pieces to strike.

Surrounding the will are aspects which "decorate" the morally good act, just as the pieces of the chime surround the disk. These aspects are those significant to any moral judgment: time, place, manner, circumstances. They are required in any moral judgment and without them the will could never function as a rational will. Like the chime, the morally good act exhibits both a visual and musical beauty. It is pleasing to the eye and ear. This aesthetic perspective informs all other aspects of the moral discussion. It offers the whole against which each piece is to be judged. The virtues, as natural inclinations, surround the will and enhance the beauty of the will's activity. They resemble larger pieces of the wind chime, whose deep tonal beauty intensify the harmonic beauty of the music which comes forth. They are not in the center of the discussion, yet the will could not function properly without them. As natural, they assist the will without overriding the will's internal freedom.

The movement of the chime and the beautiful sound fulfill the purpose for which the chime was made. The intellectual virtue of prudence and the theological virtue of charity both belong to the nature of the will. The activity of proper moral decision-making is made possible by the balance already within the will and present in the order which surrounds it. Prudence is the practical wisdom which perceives and creates moral goodness as a work of art. Charity completes the practical dynamic by informing all with love. Together, prudence and charity fulfill the rational and affective dimensions of the will and await the divine response of *acceptatio*.

Together, the human goods of balance and harmony constitute that inner peace which gives rise to joy within the heart of the formed moral agent. Like the artist, she has an internal center of balance. Like the chime, his movements are graceful and grace-filled. The chime is sensitive to the slightest wind. So, too, the moral expert acts quickly in light of what circumstances demand. The greatest danger to moral living is the *non velle*, the capacity of the will to refrain from doing what is right. Moral inertia is difficult to overcome, just as physical inertia is an obstacle to movement. The dancer who has not continued to rehearse experiences stiffness in her limbs. The moral agent who delays acting finds it more difficult to respond at all.

The internal balance and external harmony of the chime correspond to the subjective and objective dimensions of moral living. Within the will, the two affections are held in a balance appropriate to the object of loving. This balance is necessary so that the affection for justice can succeed in directing the affection for possession. The harmony of goodness produced in moral activity is judged in light of rational principles and in light of the divine will. These offer appropriate means by which the will develops its ability to exercise rational deliberation in particular instances.

Rationality and Practical Wisdom

The intricate balance of affection, principle, virtue and concrete living is attained through the virtue of prudence, practical wisdom. Prudence is the practical manifestation of the will's native affection for justice: the exercise of rationality within concrete decisions. Like the artist, the prudent person has achieved a high level of expertise through years of training and reflection upon the art of living. The fullness of moral rationality is the expression of appropriate and right loving: the correct balance between concern for self and attention to others.

For Scotus, such moral expertise is not simply the result of good training within a moral community, nor is it the correct deduction of what to do, given the fundamental moral principles. It requires attention to the particular and morally relevant aspects of a given situation, in light of past experience and a fundamental grasp of basic human values as they are expressed in principles. Moral maturity requires rational attention to all aspects of a situation, in light of fundamental human goods. Such rational attention is not intermittent to the life of the experienced moral agent, but rather unifies all living around concern for right loving.

As a virtue within the intellect, prudence has access to the double cognitional activity of abstraction and intuition. Moral reasoning joins the domains of generalized principle with the concrete particular in a manner which is *sui generis*. The union of principle and virtue in the concrete situation is guided by a sense of moral beauty, a vision of the whole, and a desire to promote wholeness in personal action. Prudence guides the will in moral action which is productive of beauty and formative of character. The integrating activity of prudence is especially important for moral living. The internal concern for character expresses itself particularly in consistency of choices around basic values and in the moral focus of an orientation toward right loving. As it expresses the self-reflective rationality of the will, prudence perfects the motivation beneath moral action. The activity of practical wisdom unifies moral living around the goal of rationality and self-control.

But, just as no amount of moral training determines a decision, the judgment of prudence does not take away the freedom within the will: a freedom to refrain from action. This moment of hiatus between the conclusions about what should be done and the active undertaking of the action provides a split-second for individual freedom. This important pause ensures the rationality of the will in its ability to restrain itself. It offers the possibility to refrain from right action. There is no second nature to be found in moral living. Even the experienced moral agent is capable of error, even the saint capable of sin. In addition, this moment offers the vicious person a chance to re-think compliance with the judgment of corrupted practical reasoning. The opportunity for conversion is located at the level of human rationality and self-control.

Prudence as practical wisdom is the guiding manifestation of rationality within moral living. It assists in moral deliberation about external action and informs reflection upon moral motivation. It governs the domain of virtue and moral inclination. Prudence involves the human art of attention to the particular in light of larger considerations. It works with the will to integrate human action around the activity of right loving.

Mutuality and Relational Living

Scotus's moral perspective offers an important basis from which to approach a number of areas of contemporary discussion. The essential order constitutes a relational order which joins all beings to God. The natural order, along with the free, has value as part of the whole gift which creation represents for the believer, and particularly for the Christian. If, as human persons, we were not naturally related to God as creatures, we could never be capable of entering into free relationship of mutuality. The affirmation of goodness in all being and the emphasis upon respect for creation as a divine gift has particular relevance for environmental dimensions in a moral theory. The order of nature is one upon which all moral action depends, therefore nature is neither to be abused nor manipulated. In addition, mutuality with God results in a common view of reality: we see the world with God's eyes. The human responsibility is to care for and nurture the environment, to exercise control over the desire for domination, to curtail waste and misuse of resources. This care can take the form of an attitude of mutuality which seeks first to understand the mystery of nature and of all life. The mechanization of nature has impoverished our understanding of our own humanity. A recovery of the sacredness of all life would benefit all.

Second, the importance of mutuality among persons with creation, with one another and with God clearly has implications for personal, national and international dimensions. Personally, this means that moral living is not an individual triumph of self over self or even self over others. Moral living requires recognition that human development requires relational living. The individual does not constitute himself. A graphic example of this is seen in the medical phenomenon of "failure to thrive" in infants. The inability of a newborn to experience relatedness to another human being, particularly the mother, results in death. Both spiritual and psychological writers affirm that the full development of an individual as a person requires a context of relatedness and love. This insight is so significant for Scotus and all Christian writers, that the discussion of the Trinity has developed around it. The self is a person only in relation to another person.

For the community of persons, this implies that society has a responsibility to promote a moral community in which values are sustained, persons are respected and life is defended. The need for moral communities is increasingly felt today, as the fragmentation of the social fabric results in civic communities which are concerned to arm themselves at alarming rates. The increase of violent crime gives tragic testimony to a civilization in decline. This decline is reflected in the rise of suicide rates, especially among the young who are exposed to horrors every time they leave their homes and who live lives of quiet despair. For many, there is no hope, no future, no reason to live. As Viktor Frankl has so poignantly written, the meaning in life is discovered only through and in loving another person or creating a work of art.[8] These two acts are so similar to the central themes of Scotus's writings that it leads me to conclude that his thought, if more widely known, would indeed contribute significantly to contemporary moral discussion.

On the international level, mutuality means a better cooperation among those nations which produce the goods for consumption and those which consume them. The imbalance between the first and third worlds, and the rapid development of the fourth world (poverty within industrialized countries) is the result of a flagrant rejection of moral values. The disproportionate consumption of the goods of the earth by a fraction of its inhabitants cannot be morally justified. Insofar as multi-national corporations defy regulation and promote exploitation of poorer peoples the situation will only worsen. Such lack of proper distribution runs counter to the moral goal. Profit-dominated capitalism does not promote relationships of cooperation and friendship but stimulates competition. Too often this results in large takeovers and, ultimately, the elimination of the competition which is the basis for the free market.

If mutuality is the moral goal, then all persons have a right to share equally in all goods. Private property is not an absolute right. The use of goods takes second place to the value of persons. National policies which treat persons as objects run counter to the creation of a truly moral society. A Christian moral vision must continue to speak to such a world, to denounce systems of exploitation and dominance. This moral vision must embrace the central message of the Gospel: love and forgiveness. It must work with all of good will to promote the values of life, respect and care for all persons. It must seek non-violent means to influence and change unjust conditions. It must speak to all, the poor as well as the rich, the simple as well as the learned, the humble as well as the powerful.

---

[8]   Viktor Frankl, *Man's Search for Meaning*, Washington Square Press 1984, pp. 55-63.

The message of Scotus is the Gospel, writ large and in a language for the learned. It is, however, also the message of Francis of Assisi, the Poverello. As each generation seeks to find a language for the message of Jesus, we must work to rediscover the wealth of the Christian Scholastic tradition. The medieval affirmation of the whole and of the cosmic order provides a response to the contemporary moral fragmentation. Scotus is one voice within that tradition. His is not the only voice, but it is a voice which has not been heard to the same degree as his famous predecessor, Thomas Aquinas. As a thinker whose insights delighted such men as Gerard Manley Hopkins and Pierre Teilhard de Chardin, Scotus may have a message to join poet and scientist together in a vision of reality as manifestation of divine love.

We can learn much from Scotus's presentation of the moral life. When moral excellence is not primarily an intellectual achievement, but rather the perfection of selfless love, then the human heart is called to do what it does best: respond rationally to what is good. Self-controlled rational love is the highest moral response. In a universe created freely out of a divine act of rational love, a universe overflowing with goodness, the human will moves gradually toward better and better choices about the many goods which surround it. To be a moral agent for Scotus is to develop continually the ability to love in an orderly manner. For this perfection, the will is naturally and rationally well-equipped.

bibliography

Iohannis Duns Scotus. *Opera.* Civitas Vaticana: Typis polyglottis Vaticanis 1950-1993.

Iohannis Duns Scotus. *Opera Omnia.* Wadding-Vivès 1891.

> John Duns Scotus. *God and Creatures: The Quodlibetal Questions.* Translated by F. Alluntis and A.B. Wolter. Princeton: Princeton University Press. 1975.

> John Duns Scotus. *A Treatise on God as First Principle.* Translated and edited by Allan B. Wolter. Chicago: Franciscan Herald Press. 1966.

Aertsen, Jan. "Beauty in the Middle Ages: A Forgotten Transcendental?". *Medieval Philosophy and Theology.* 1 (1991), 68-97.

Aubenque, Pierre. "La <Phronésis> chez les Stoiciens". *La Prudence chez Aristote.* Paris: PUF 1986, 184-5.

Austen, Jane. *Pride and Prejudice.* Barnes and Noble. 1993.

Bellah, Robert *et al. Habits of the Heart.* Berkeley: University of California Press 1985.

Bettoni, Ephrem. *Duns Scotus: Basic Principles of His Philosophy.* Washington: Catholic University Press 1961.

Boler, John. "Transcending the Natural: Duns Scotus on the Two Affections of the Will. *American Catholic Philosophical Quarterly.* 67 (1993), 109-126.

Borak, A. "Libertà e prudenza nel pensiero di Duns Scoto". *Laurentianum* 10 (1969), 105-141.

Day, Sebastian. *Intuitive Cognition: a Key to the Later Scholastics.* St. Bonaventure: Franciscan Institute Press. 1947.

Dod, Bernard G. "Aristoteles latinus". *The Cambridge History of Later Medieval Philosophy.* Kretzmann, Kenny, Pinborg (ed.). Cambridge University Press 1982, 45-79.

Dumont, Richard. "Intuition: Prescript or Postscript to Scotus' Demonstration of God's Existence". *Deus et Homo ad Mentem I. Duns Scoti.* Rome. 1972, 81-87.

Frank, William. "Duns Scotus' Concept of Willing Freely: What Divine Freedom Beyond Choice Teaches Us". *Franciscan Studies.* 42 (1982), 68-89.

Frankl, Viktor. *Man's Search for Meaning.* Washington Square Press 1984.

Gilson, Etienne. "Avicenne et le point de départ de Duns Scot". *Archives d'Histoire Doctrinale et Littéraire du Moyen Age.* 1927, 89-150.

Glendon, Mary Ann. *Rights Talk: The Impoverishment of Political Discourse.* New York: MacMillan 1991.

Grisez, Germain. *The Way of the Lord Jesus.* Franciscan Herald Press 1983.

Hissette, Roland. *Enquête sur les 219 articles condamnés à Paris le 7 mars 1277.* Louvain-Paris 1977.

Honnefelder, Ludger. *Ens Inquantum Ens. Der Begriff des Seienden als solchen als Gegenstand der Metaphysik nach der Lehre des Johannes Duns Scotus.* Münster: Aschendorff. 1979.

Honnefelder, Ludger. "Die Kritik des Johannes Duns Scotus am kosmologischen Nezessitarismus der Araber: Ansätze zu einem neuen Frieheitsbegriff". *Die abendländische Freiheit vom 10. zum 14. Jahrhundert.* J. Fried (Hrsg.). Sigmaringen 1991, 249-263.

Ingham, Mary Elizabeth. "The Condemnation of 1277: Another Light on Scotist Ethics". *Freiburger Zeitschrift für Theologie und Philosophie.* 37 (1990), 91-103.

Ingham, Mary Elizabeth. "Scotus and the Moral Order". *American Catholic Philosophical Quarterly.* 67 (1993), 127-150.

Ingham, Mary Elizabeth. "John Duns Scotus: An Integrated Vision". *The History of Franciscan Theology.* Edited by Kenan B. Osborne, OFM. St. Bonaventure: The Franciscan Institute 1994. 185-230.

Kent, Bonnie. *Aristotle and the Franciscans: Gerald Odonis' Commentary on the Nicomachean Ethics.* Unpublished Ph.D. dissertation 1984.

Kluxen, Wolfgang. "Welterfahrung und Gottesbeweis: eine Studie zum "Tractatus de Primo Principio" des Johannes Duns Scotus". *Deus et Homo ad Mentem I. Duns Scoti.* Rome. 1972, 47-59.

Kovach, Francis. "Divine and Human Beauty in Duns Scotus' Philosophy and Theology". *Deus et Homo ad Mentem I. Duns Scoti.* Rome 1972, 445-459. Reprinted in *Scholastic Challenges to Some Mediaeval and Modern Ideas.* 1987.

Lottin, Odon. *Psychologie et morale aux XIIe et XIIIe siècles.* Gembloux 1957.

MacIntyre, Alasdaire. *After Virtue.* Notre Dame Press 1981, 1986.

Martin, Christopher. *The Philosophy of Thomas Aquinas.* London: Routledge 1989.

Messner, Reinhold Oswald. "Die Ökumenische Bedeutung der Skotischen Trinitätslehre". *De Doctrina I. Duns Scoti.* Rome 1968. III, 653-726.

Mulvaney, Robert J. "Wisdom, Time and Avarice in St. Thomas Aquinas's Treatment on Prudence". *The Modern Schoolman.* 69 (March/May 1992), 443–462.

Nederman, Cary. "Nature, Ethics and the Doctrine of *Habitus.* Aristotelian Moral Psychology in the Twelfth Century". *Traditio.* 45 (1989–90), 87–110.

Nelson, Daniel Mark. *The Priority of Prudence.* Penn State Press 1992.

Nussbaum, Martha. *The Fragility of Goodness.* Cambridge University Press 1987.

Prentice, Robert. "The Contingent Element Governing the Natural Law on the Last Seven Precepts of the Decalogue, According to Duns Scotus". *Antonianum.* 42 (1967), 259–292.

Van der Walt, B.J. "Regnum Hominis et Regnum Dei: Historical-Critical Discussion of the Relationship between Nature and Supernature According to Duns Scotus". *Regnum hominis et Regnum Dei,* Rome 1976. I, 219–229.

van Steenberghen, Fernand. "La philosophie à la veille de l'entrée de Jean Duns Scot". *De Doctrina I. Duns Scoti.* Rome 1968, I, 65–74.

Verbeke, Gérard. *The Presence of Stoicism in Medieval Thought.* Washington: Catholic University Press 1983.

Vignaux, Paul. *Justification et prédestination au XIVe siècle.* Paris 1934.

Vignaux, Paul. "Lire Duns Scot Aujourd'hui". *Regnum hominis et regnum Dei.* Rome 1976, 33–46.

Vignaux, Paul. "Valeur morale et valeur de salut". *Homo et Mundus.* Rome 1984, 53–67.

Vignaux, Paul. "Métaphysique de l'Exode, philosophie de la religion (A Partir du *De Primo Principio* selon Duns Scot)". *Rivista de Filosofia neo-scolastica.* 70 (1978), 135–148.

von Balthasar, Hans Urs. *The Glory of the Lord.* San Francisco: Ignatius Press 1989.

Wieland, Georg. *Ethica: Scientia Practica.* Münster:Aschendorff 1981.

Wieland, Georg. "The Reception of Aristotle's Ethics". *Cambridge History of Later Medieval Philosophy.* 657–672.

Wieland, Georg. "Happiness: The Perfection of Man". *Cambridge History of Later Medieval Philosophy.* 673–686.

Wolter, Allan B. *The Transcendentals and Their Function in the Metaphysics of Duns Scotus.* Franciscan Institute. 1946.

Wolter, Allan B. *The Philosophical Theology of John Duns Scotus.* Marilyn McCord Adams (editor). Ithaca: Cornell University Press, 1990.

Wolter, Allan B. *Duns Scotus on the Will and Morality.* Washington: Catholic University of America Press, 1986.

Wolter, Allan B. *Duns Scotus' Early Oxford Lecture on Individuation.* Santa Barbara, CA: Old Mission, 1992.

Wolter, Allan B. *Duns Scotus' Political and Economic Philosophy.* Santa Barbara, CA: Old Mission, 1989.

Wolter, Allan B. *Four Questions on Mary.* Santa Barbara, CA: Old Mission, 1988.

Indices

Index of Terms

Index of Names

DATE DUE

			Printed in USA